Your Kingdom Come

j.john

A group study of
the Lord's Prayer
in ten sessions

MONARCH
BOOKS

Mill Hill, London and Grand Rapids, Michigan

First published by Monarch Books in the UK in 2001,
Concorde House, Grenville Place, Mill Hill, London NW7 3SA.

Distributed by:
UK: STL, PO Box 300, Kingstown Broadway,
Carlisle, Cumbria CA3 0QS;
USA: Kregel Publications, PO Box 2607,
Grand Rapids, Michigan 49501.

ISBN 1 85424 550 3 (UK)
ISBN 0 8254 6039 5 (USA)

British Library Cataloguing Data
A catalogue record for this book is available
from the British Library.

Book design and production for the publishers by
Gazelle Creative Productions Ltd,
Concorde House, Grenville Place, Mill Hill, London NW7 3SA.

ACKNOWLEDGEMENTS

I owe a debt of gratitude to Dr Chris Walley, my collaborator on this book. Chris shaped my thinking, challenged my ideas and got my creative juices flowing.

I would like to thank my wife Killy and her Bible Study group: Lis Hawkins, Kath Grant, Kathy Cleveland, Louise Dyer and Jane Bradnock, who piloted these studies. Your feedback was perceptive and helpful in refining the studies.

Thank you to Tony Collins, my publisher, who believed in this book from the beginning – thank you for your support, encouragement and enthusiasm for these studies.

And finally, I am especially thankful to God for giving me a life worth living, a faith worth believing and a Saviour worth knowing.

CONTENTS

CONTENTS

Introduction

INTRODUCTION

This book is a series of ten studies on the Lord's Prayer; Jesus Christ's brief summary on prayer for his followers. If you are someone who prays, or someone who is at least prepared to consider the possibility that prayer is important, then I am certain that you will find studying this prayer of enormous value.

In this introduction I want to explain why prayer is so important, to outline the basis of these studies and to make some brief comments about how to get the best out of them. In an appendix at the end of the book I have added some advice for group leaders.

The Reason for these Studies

We can define prayer simply as "communication with God". One part of prayer is us talking to God and sharing with him our thoughts, feelings, hopes and fears. The other part of prayer is us listening to him.

The Lord's Prayer is Jesus Christ's summary on how his followers are to pray. In my book *God's Priorities, Living Life from the Lord's Prayer* (Kingsway, 2001), which gives the background to these studies, I have given a number of reasons why prayer is so important. Let me summarize them here.

1) Prayer, especially praise in prayer, glorifies God

God deserves our praise; he is the creator of all things. Can you imagine a stunning concert where no one clapped at the end? What an injustice! Yet not to praise God for all the good things we see, hear and feel every day would be an even greater injustice.

2) Prayer allows us to be involved in God's actions in the world

God doesn't need our prayers in order for him to act; after all he is the almighty Lord of the universe. Yet in prayer, God draws us into the working out of the great plan of history. As a consequence of prayer, empires fall, history changes course, evil is curbed and good is brought out of apparent disaster.

3) Prayer allows us to enjoy fellowship with God by communicating with him

Through prayer our relationship with God develops. Prayer is the process where our lives put down roots into the infinite riches of God. Without prayer, any spiritual life we have will wither away.

4) Prayer allows us to receive God's priorities for our lives

We live in a culture where there is a vast range of forces that are seeking to push us away from God and to steer our lives off the right course. All the time there is a strong and constant pressure for us to adopt the priorities of our culture, not those of God. Prayer, especially that vital part of prayer where we listen to God, allows us to find where we are and to see where we should be going. Prayer allows us to get our lives back on course.

Most Christians know that prayer is important and that is why they often feel unhappy about the quality of their prayer life. However, many go on to make a serious mistake; they think that they can do nothing to improve how they pray. Many Christians (and probably many other people too) think that the ability to pray is something like a sense of pitch or rhythm; you either have it or you haven't.

Yet from Luke's account of the giving of the Lord's Prayer, we learn a remarkable thing. It is this: there are aspects to praying that can be taught and learned. In Luke 11:1–2 we read this: "Once when Jesus had been out praying, one of his disciples came to him as he finished and said, 'Lord, teach us to pray, just as John taught his disciples.' He said, 'This is how you should pray: Our Father....'" And Jesus goes on to give them the Lord's Prayer. You get the picture? This disciple, impressed by how Jesus prays, asks to be taught how to pray. And Jesus doesn't reply with a shrug of the shoulders and some dismissive words to the effect that "Prayer is a gift" or "Good praying is caught, not taught." He says, in effect, "OK, this is the pattern. Now listen carefully." Of course, Jesus is not giving a formula; everything in his teaching on prayer tells us that praying must be centred on a spiritual relationship, not ritual techniques. And, as we shall see, if you are not in a right relationship with Christ, then no amount of study will help your prayers. The good news on prayer, however (and remember it comes from Jesus, the most reliable source of information you can get), is this: our praying can be improved.

Actually, this ought not to be a surprise. Most human relationships, whether those at work, leisure or within our families, can be enhanced if we work at them. That is why we have counselling for marriage and for the workplace; there are bad habits we can remove and good habits we can acquire. Prayer— the spiritual relationship the Christian has with God—is no different. A careful, thoughtful study of the Lord's Prayer can change how we pray.

Yet the significance of the Lord's Prayer goes way beyond how we pray. In its brief span, it covers literally every area of existence. Quite simply, how we pray determines how we live. The pattern of how to pray given by Jesus is something that can have revolutionary consequences.

Working through the Lord's Prayer for these books, I have been astonished at how deep and wide-ranging the teaching within this prayer is. For all its brevity and familiarity, this prayer casts a brilliant (though sometimes uncomfortable) light on how we live our lives. If any part of the Bible deserves detailed and careful study, it is this.

Why a Small-group Bible Study?

While it is easy to agree that the Lord's Prayer is important, you may well ask whether a small-group study is necessary? Why shouldn't you and I simply sit down with this book and work through these exercises on our own? Well, we could do just that. Yet the experience of many generations of Christians is that one of the most effective ways of studying the Bible is as part of a small group.

Let me give you some reasons why small-group study is so effective.

First (and perhaps foremost), a small-group Bible study can engage us in a deeper way than a book or sermon. Reading a book or hearing a sermon are passive activities. We sit and read (or sit and listen) and the danger is that we are only affected superficially. In that case, what we hear or read, like the seed on the hard ground in Jesus' story of the sower (Matthew 13:4,19), may soon be uprooted. As spectators, we do not always engage with the challenge of God's word and all too often we soon forget what was said or what we have read. A Bible study, because it is interactive and makes us participants, works at a more profound level. Through a Bible study the seed of God's word is planted deeper and as a result we can be more effectively and permanently changed by it.

Second, I believe that small-group Bible study is especially good for encouraging virtues that can be in short supply when we study the Bible on our own.

- The presence of the questions and the interaction with other people forces us to *perseverance* in understanding hard passages. On our own, it is all too easy to give up on difficult or demanding passages and to move on. In a study group there is normally someone to say, "Yes but *why* does this passage say that?"
- The act of answering questions and expressing those answers publicly encourages *clarity*. We are forced to express what we think the passage means and in doing so we have to come to terms with what the passage is actually saying. Equally, the viewpoints of other people can make us see a Bible passage afresh. We may decide that the view that we have always held is wrong.
- Above all perhaps, small-group Bible study forces us to be *honest* with ourselves. If, for example, we glance at Jesus' command for us "not to be like the hypocrites" (Matthew 6:5), on our own it is all too easy to shrug our shoulders, say, "no problem," and dismiss the passage on the basis that we are not hypocrites and that the Pharisees are extinct. In a small group though you are quite likely to hear someone say, "Wait a minute, couldn't this also apply to us if we pretend that we are more spiritual than we really are?" Of course, this means that a study group can sometimes be slightly uncomfortable. However, if the discomfort comes from the word of God speaking into our lives through the Holy Spirit, then we should welcome it.

The Basis of these Studies

In this book there are ten studies on the Lord's Prayer and the teaching on prayer which precedes it in Matthew 6:5–13. As the Lord's Prayer is a summary of the teaching of Jesus and the Bible on prayer, I have used the prayer itself as a framework from which to look at other Bible passages relevant to the topics that it covers. In addition to looking at the Lord's Prayer itself I have also included two important preliminary studies that look at the teaching on how we pray that Jesus gives in Matthew 6:5–8. Matthew 7:7–11 (which in the *New Living Bible* is entitled *Effective Prayer*) is so closely linked to Jesus' teaching on prayer in Matthew 6 that I have included it in Study 2.

Let me also explain the sort of studies that I have aimed to produce. There are many types of Bible study. Some studies use tightly focused questions with a single right answer to trace a well-marked path from which no deviation is allowed. Their advantages are those of microwave meals; they are easily prepared and they are relatively foolproof. Their disadvantages are, however, also those of microwave meals: they tend to be bland and unmemorable and they often don't suit the needs of your particular group. In reality a 'one-size-fits-all' Bible study never really fits anybody.

These studies are different. Many of the questions are designed to elicit thought and reflection rather than a "yes" or "no" answer. In fact I believe that the best sort of Bible study is not simply about getting right answers to questions. It is actually about training people to get those answers themselves. It is helping people to get into good habits of reading the Bible and applying it to their lives. A Bible study is not about feeding sheep, it is training sheep to feed themselves and, ultimately, to train other sheep.

My personal conviction is that the Lord's Prayer *is* challenging and that Jesus intended it to be this way. Sadly, twenty centuries of frequently careless and often mindless repetition have dulled the impact of the Lord's Prayer. The result is that there is a danger that when we think of it we think of something bland, gentle and calming; a sort of Valium of the soul. I passionately believe that this is actually completely counter to Jesus' intention; the Lord's Prayer was designed to wake us up and motivate us for action, not soothe us to sleep!

These studies are therefore designed to force us to think about exactly what the Lord's Prayer means and what its implications are for the way we live.

I have put the main instructions for leaders at the end of this book. Here though let me say that as all study groups differ I have built a considerable degree of flexibility into these studies. I have provided more material here than the average group will use so that the leaders can pick and choose what they feel is appropriate for their particular setting. In at least three of the studies (4, 6 and 8) the material could, with profit, be spread over two weeks.

To facilitate this flexibility I have put tick boxes by the main units so that leaders can mark the ones they actually plan to use. I have indicated my own preference on which material is critical by putting ◉ next to those passages that I feel can't be omitted without distorting the study. Unmarked material can be considered as more optional. The existence of this flexibility does mean that the leader has to work harder. Be warned!

In a separate section at the end of each study I have put supplementary material. The extent to which you use this material depends on how long your group spends on each study. If you have a group that moves quickly through the set passages then I suggest that the leader has some of the supplementary material ready. Some people may also find it helpful as "homework" or as a source for private study. Group members can also use the tick boxes to mark material that they have studied so that they can study the rest in their own time.

With respect to Bible versions these questions were written around the text of the *New Living Translation* (British text: Tyndale UK, 2000), but they have also been checked against the *New International Version*. Either version is satisfactory and probably most modern translations (such as NRSV and GNB) will also work well. Although I have a great deal of respect for the King James (or Authorized) Version, I find that in small-group Bible study it tends to be distracting because so much effort goes into simply trying to understand the language. I make some further comments on Bible versions in the Appendix.

Finally I want to mention here that I have made a deliberate policy of directing the studies to a number of Old Testament prayers. I have done this for several reasons.

- First, Jesus and the disciples were Jews and the prayers of the Old Testament would have been extremely familiar to them. The prayers of people like Abraham, David and Hannah would have been their patterns of how to pray.
- Second, I think it is important to realize that Jesus did not come to overturn the practices of the Old Testament spirituality. Jesus' criticisms of the "prayer hypocrites" were actually directed at people *not* because they prayed according to the Old Testament pattern but because they didn't. They had distorted the way prayer ought to be. When it came to prayer, Jesus was as much a reformer as a revolutionary.
- Third, a danger of studying the New Testament on its own is that that we overlook the previous two-thirds of the Bible. 2 Timothy 3:16 begins, "All Scripture is inspired by God and is useful to teach us..." and that "all" includes the Old Testament. We read that Jesus said to the disciples, "Every teacher of religious law who has become a disciple in the Kingdom of Heaven is like a person who brings out of the storehouse the new teachings as well as the old" (Matthew 13:52). The challenge Jesus was making to his hearers was for them to take hold of the new teachings; the challenge he makes to us here is not to lose the ancient teachings.
- Fourth, there are, quite simply, some wonderful prayers in the Old Testament. There are prayers of joy and prayers of despair, prayers that are complex and prayers that are simple, prayers that have been carefully thought about and prayers that are spontaneous. The Old Testament is a great scrapbook of prayers (and pray-ers); neglecting it is unwise.

Study Elements

Each study is divided into the following components: The suggested timings are based around an 80 to 90-minute study time. I have put some more advice on these sections for those leading the study in the Appendix.

Starter

This is a short warm-up activity. It is designed to put everybody at ease and to get them talking. This should take no more than ten minutes.

Surgery

This section focuses in on some of the problems that this part of the Lord's Prayer addresses. Again, I would expect this to take no more than ten minutes.

Study

This is the heart of the material and is the one that occupies most of the time. This section generally includes two sorts of passages to study. The first of these are the essential sections and are marked with ◉, the second are less important. There is also supplementary material provided at the end of the study; whether or not this is used is up to the group leader. Anything not covered in the study can be studied later at your leisure. This study section should take a maximum of 60 minutes.

Summary

This is a short review section which tries to bring together some of the conclusions that have emerged during the study. For this section I would recommend that you allow ten minutes.

Stepping out

This is the *so what?* section. It is a series of suggestions, thoughts and questions to try and encourage the application of what has been learnt. Christianity is not simply about knowing the right answers; it is about doing right actions. This section also includes suggestions for further study material. In one sense, completing this section will take between five and ten minutes. In another sense, it will take you a life-time!

Practicalities

Leading and participating in a Bible study are two different things. I have given out a sort of brief do-it-yourself guide to starting and leading a Bible study in the Appendix. Here my comments are for those who are participating in the study. Even if you have been doing Bible studies for years I would still urge you to read these through and think about them. My advice can be summarized under the three great biblical words: faith, truth and love.

Have faith

There is a time and a place for hard questions about the nature of the Bible text (Can I believe this? Are our translations correct? etc), but a Bible study is not it. The traditional Christian belief is that when we have a Bible in our hands what we hold is God's written word to us, inspired and preserved by the power of the Holy Spirit. We profit most from Bible study if we believe that this is indeed God's word and that in it God speaks to us. In a Bible study it is not us that judges the text, it is the text that judges us. This position of faith in the text is not naive credulity ("just believe"), it is a position that can (and has been) carefully and thoughtfully argued. It also has its own internal logic; after all, no interaction with a person is going to be successful unless there is some degree of trust in his or her truthfulness. If you do have a question though don't sit on it; find a Christian whose knowledge and judgement you trust and ask them about it. Alternatively, there are almost certainly excellent books available on the problem. Your church leader or a Christian bookshop may be able to point you in the right direction.

Have honesty

Bible studies like these deal with real-life issues (like forgiveness) and as such they can get painfully close to the bone. Be careful that you do not slip into the classic defence of human beings when faced with a moral challenge—deciding that it only applies to other people. So be watchful that you do not encourage a discussion about greed perhaps, to centre on how a particular class of people (say, bankers or builders) are thieves. Unless we are bankers or builders ourselves, this sort of thing only makes us feel smug. Be honest with yourself and let the light shine in the dark places of your life. Of course, being honest is not the same as blurting out your deepest and darkest secrets. You may find that there will be times when you prefer to keep silent. The good study group and the wise study leader should both expect and respect a desire for privacy. It is, however, absolutely critical that you are both open and honest with God.

Have love

This is most important.

- Think of others in your group all the time. Let them speak, encourage them and where you can build on their comments.
- Be sensitive to the wounds that others may have. For instance, it is very easy to say, "You just have to forgive!" For people who have suffered appalling physical or psychological hurts, forgiveness may not be an easy option at all. Think before you speak, lest your words hurt those who are already wounded.
- Don't be critical of others, even when you know they are wrong.
- Treat what has emerged in these meetings in total confidence.
- Between studies, pray for those that meet with you around God's word.

The Layout of these Studies

1. Preliminary 1: Praying for the right reason.
2. Preliminary 2: Praying in the right way.
3. Privilege 1: Praying to our Father...
4. Privilege 2: Having a heavenly Father and an earthly family.
5. Praise: Honouring God's name as holy.
6. Purpose: Knowing the meaning of life.
7. Provision: Asking for what God wants to give us.
8. Pardon: Being a forgiven and forgiving people.
9. Protection: Battling against evil.
10. Perspective: Living life God's way.

Text Conventions

The following basic conventions are used in the text:

◉ A vital passage.

❑ Tick box, for marking material you plan to do, or have done.

Note: Italicized text like this is a general comment either on the background to the passage or on some issue raised by it.

Leader's note: Boxed text like this is a comment mainly for the benefit of leaders.

STUDY 1

Preliminary 1: Praying for the right reason

"And now about prayer. When you pray, don't be like the hypocrites who love to pray publicly on street corners and in the synagogues where everyone can see them. I assure you, that is all the reward they will ever get. But when you pray, go away by yourself, shut the door behind you, and pray to your Father secretly. Then your Father, who knows all secrets, will reward you."
(Matthew 6:5,6 [NLT])

INTRODUCTION

The Lord's Prayer occurs in Matthew's Gospel as part of a long section of teaching (Matthew 5:1 – 7:27) that has become known as the "Sermon on the Mount" because of the reference (in Matthew 5:1) that it was given by Jesus to his disciples on a hill. It occurs in a shortened form in Luke 11. The prayer itself (Matthew 6:9–13) is prefaced by a short passage (verses 5–8) where Jesus teaches about the basics of prayer. This study looks at what Jesus teaches about praying for the right reason.

1) STARTER

Discuss *some* of the following:

1) If you could have a day's free coaching by an expert in some sport, hobby or skill, who would you choose? Why?

2) Ask *volunteers* to talk briefly about their most successful attempt at pretending to be someone they were not.

3) Can someone give an illustration from a TV or radio "soap" where someone is abusing a friendship for their own purposes? How do you feel about it?

4) Has anybody ever done something they disliked (eg, gone to a football match, smoked, watched opera or eaten sushi) purely to impress someone else? ❏

2) SURGERY

Discuss *some* of the following:

1) *Either* How would you feel if your prayers were broadcast publicly? *or* Who is satisfied with their prayer life?

2) Have you ever admired someone else's prayers? Why?

3) Do you prefer written or off-the-cuff, spontaneous prayers in church? What are the positives and negatives of both?

4) Should public prayers come from the head or the heart?   ❑

3) STUDY

This is divided into two parts:

Part 1: An Old Testament Prayer

Most of the ninety or so prayers in the Bible come from those books that make up the Old Testament. These prayers, from Abraham, Moses, Hannah, David, Jeremiah, Nehemiah and many others, would have been the handbook of prayer for both Jesus and his disciples. Many of the Psalms in particular are prayers of either an individual or a community. Psalm 13 is a good short example of an intense personal prayer. A study of two more Old Testament prayers is given in the Supplementary Material at the end of the study.

◉ **Read Psalm 13.**
For the choir director: A psalm of David.

Note: a) The title of this psalm is ambiguous: it could mean "written for David", "to David" or "by David". The most natural reading (adopted here) is that King David was the author; b) The word translated as the LORD is not just a title: it represents the personal name of God in the Old Testament. This name (probably pronounced Yahweh) is particularly associated with the solemn binding agreement (or covenant) that God established in Old Testament times with his people Israel. In this covenant God promised to look after his people and to bless them with "an unfailing love" (see verse 5).

1) What reasons does David have for praying?
2) What sort of frame of mind do you think David was in for him to pray like this? What emotions does this prayer express? At the beginning? At the end?
3) What is the basis of David's hope that the LORD will answer him?
4) What do you think a prayer like this says about David's relationship to God?
5) Although this prayer is recorded in the Book of Psalms is it really a public prayer? If someone got up in church and prayed a prayer like this, how would you feel? Would you be embarrassed? Why?
6) This prayer reflects David's response to a tough situation. Is this style of intimate personal prayer only appropriate for bad times?
7) What lessons can we learn from this psalm about how we should pray?   ❑

Part 2: Jesus' warning about praying for the wrong reasons

⊙ **Read Matthew 6:1–18.**

1) Look at verses 2, 5 and 16. What three aspects of "being religious" is Jesus addressing?

2) In each case Jesus warns against "hypocrites". In the Greek of Jesus' day the word "*hypocrites*" referred to "someone who acted out a part in a play". Looking at verses 1–18, answer the following questions:

   a) Where is the place that these "hypocrites" carry out their religion? Where, in contrast, does Jesus say his followers should carry it out?

   b) What is the motive for the religion of the "hypocrites"? What, in contrast, does Jesus say the motives of his followers should be?

   c) What reward will the "hypocrites" receive from other people? What, in contrast, does Jesus say is the reward that his followers will receive from them?

   d) What reward will the "hypocrites" receive from God? What, in contrast, does Jesus say is the reward that his followers will receive from God?

   e) What description of God is given here three times?

3) The English word "hypocrite" is such a negative word that we rarely ever admit it might apply to ourselves. Our use of the word tends to be in the following form: "*He* is a hypocrite, *you* are inconsistent, *I* just set myself impossible ideals." When we think of "a religious hypocrite" we think of someone who *intentionally* sets out to deceive others. Yet a more subtle (and perhaps unintentional) play-acting is also possible and probably more common. Let's look specifically at Jesus' words about praying in verses 5–6:

   ⊙ "And now about prayer. When you pray, don't be like the hypocrites who love to pray publicly on street corners and in the synagogues where everyone can see them. I assure you, that is all the reward they will ever get. But when you pray, go away by yourself, shut the door behind you, and pray to your Father secretly. Then your Father, who knows all secrets, will reward you."

   a) Public outdoors praying is not common in our society. Why, in Jesus' time and culture, might people have wanted to do this?

   b) Think about these "prayer play-actors". Who are they really praying to? How do you think they became like this?

   c) How is this sort of prayer different from that practised by David in Psalm 13?

   d) How might we be tempted to have a counterfeit prayer life?

   e) In Matthew's Gospel, Jesus specifically condemns hypocrisy eleven times. Why do you think that Jesus felt that this sort of "spiritual play acting" was so dangerous?

   f) According to Jesus' instructions for prayer in verse 6, who are to be the only parties involved in our praying?

   g) How practically might we carry this out today? Does it rule out all public praying? (See Acts 4:24,31).

h) Is all our religion to be secret? How do we square that with Matthew 5:14–16? ❏

4) SUMMARY

a) What things do you need for a relationship to exist between two people?

b) For a close and genuine relationship to *continue* to exist between two people, what features should be characteristic of their communication? What would happen to the relationship if one of the parties started "play-acting"?

c) Look again at the passage in Matthew 6:5–6. What promise does Jesus make there to those who pray privately to the Father? ❏

5) STEPPING OUT

Practical suggestions

- Why do you pray? Because it's communicating with God? Because it's expected of you? Because it's something that Christians do? Because you feel a sense of guilt if you don't pray? On the basis of what you have just studied what do you think the answer should be?
- How can we go about changing our motives for praying?
- How do you suppose you get to be a "prayer play-actor"? How can we stop that tendency in ourselves and in others? How can we be more real with God?
- Have you ever joined in with a prayer or even prayed out loud a prayer that you didn't believe in?
- Think about how you pray. Do your prayers reflect the fact that God is listening? How can we make time for God to speak to us when we pray?
- Should we ever be concerned about what other people think of our praying? ❏

Further study

- The principle that God is concerned with what is going on in our minds not what we appear to be is spelt out in 1 Samuel 16:7.
- There are a number of intensely personal prayers recorded in the Bible. There are numerous examples in the Psalms (for example, Psalms 3–7; 25, 28, 44) and elsewhere, for example Exodus 32:7–14, 1 Kings 3:5–15.
- Hannah and Daniel are two good examples of costly public praying that are given in the Supplementary Material. ❏

Questions to think about

- If God was not personal but some kind of cosmic force (apologies to *Star Wars*), how would that affect the way we pray to him/it?
- In what ways does the relationship we have to God through prayer differ from relationships we have with people around us?
- Do you ever forget that God is a real and living God?
- In some church traditions the Lord's Prayer and other prayers are set to

music and sung. From the point of view of *prayer* (as opposed to *art*) is this a good thing?

- How do we remind ourselves that what we are doing in prayer is enjoying a relationship and not carrying out a ritual?
- Which is better: to pray genuinely to God for selfish reasons ("God help me to get better!") or to pray to God simply because it is the "expected thing" for us to do?
- Are there other areas of our Christian life where we do things because others are watching rather than for God?
- How can we ensure that all we do for God is for the glory of God and not for our own glory?
- If the basis of our relationship with God is play-acting, how likely is it that our human relationships will be frank and honest? ❏

6) SUPPLEMENTARY MATERIAL

Two Old Testament examples

Praying in front of others doesn't always impress bystanders! There are two good examples of this in the Old Testament with Hannah and Daniel.

a) Hannah's Prayer

Read 1 Samuel 1:1–18.

Note: Hannah lived around 1100 BC at one of the darkest times of the Old Testament when true faith in the LORD was threatened by widespread lawlessness and immorality.

a) What crisis drives Hannah to prayer?
b) What do we learn about how Hannah prayed? (10,13,15). What lessons are there for us?
c) What initial response does her prayer provoke? (13,14). Why is Eli's reaction tragic?
d) What does this passage suggest about the reaction that heartfelt and genuine prayer may receive from others? ❏

b) Daniel's Prayer

Read Daniel 6:1–16.

Note: Daniel was a faithful Jew exiled in pagan Babylon in the middle of the sixth century BC.

a) Did Daniel need to pray with the shutters open? Why do you think he did so?
b) If he had been the sort of "prayer play-actor" condemned by Jesus, how do you think he would have reacted to the order not to pray?
c) What does this story tell us about: a) Daniel's motives for prayer, b) the value he set on prayer, and c) the sort of reaction from others that *serious* prayer can receive? ❏

Preliminary 2: Praying in the right way

"When you pray, don't babble on and on as people of other religions do. They think their prayers are answered only by repeating their words again and again. Don't be like them, because your Father knows exactly what you need even before you ask him! Pray like this… " (Matthew 6:7–8 [NLT])

INTRODUCTION

As we noted in the last study, before giving the Lord's Prayer, Jesus gave two warnings about praying. The first of these was a warning about play-acting so that we do not pray from the wrong motives. The second warning from Jesus deals with another danger. This time though, Jesus is not concerned with *why* we pray; he is concerned with *how* we pray.

1) STARTER

Discuss *some* of the following:

a) You hear someone described as having "a good command of the English language". Do you understand this to mean that: i) they can use lots of words? or ii) they can express themselves clearly? What is the difference?

b) Who was the most effective speaker you have ever heard? What was so impressive about them? Why? Did their words have power?

c) When you phone an organization how do you respond to messages of the sort "You have reached The Extremely Elusive Company. All of our trained staff are currently busy. Please hold on. Your custom is extremely valuable to us"?

d) When have you ever been involved in a conversation where you were put off by the attitude the other person had towards you?   ❑

2) SURGERY

Discuss *some* of the following:

a) Excluding prayer, what is the most important conversation you have ever had?

b) Have you ever tried to persuade God to answer a prayer over something?

c) Have you ever prayed about some problem on the basis that "well I may as well try praying; it can't do any harm"?

d) Have you ever rewritten an important letter? Why?

e) Have you ever felt you were praying to empty air?   ❏

3) STUDY

This is divided into three parts, all of which are relevant to this study.

Part 1) Jesus' warning about praying the wrong way

◉ Read Matthew 6:7–8.

We need to think carefully about what exactly it is that Jesus is so critical about here.

1) Is repeating our words when we pray something always wrong?
Read Matthew 26:39,42,44.

2) Is praying for a long time something that is always wrong?
Read Luke 18:1–8.

3) So what is the problem that Jesus is addressing? Why do people babble
on and on in prayer?   ❏

Part 2) Old Testament examples of prayer

In the Old Testament we have many examples of people praying; some of them praying well and some of them praying badly.

Note: If short of time do just one of the following.

◉ a) Elijah and the prophets of Baal.
A great contrast in prayer styles can be found in the confrontation between Elijah and the prophets of Baal. The background, which is important, is that under the wicked King Ahab, instead of being loyal to the LORD, Israel has followed the pagan worship of Baal. God's prophet, Elijah, has been commanded by the LORD to bring the nation back to God.

Read 1 Kings 18:20–39.

a) Note the way the prophets of Baal pray in vv. 26–28. Why do you think they pray like this? Is this the sort of thing that Jesus was condemning?

b) Look at Elijah's prayer in vv. 36–37. In what ways is it different from
that of the prophets of Baal? What does this say about the way that Elijah
knows the LORD?   ❏

◉ **b) Abraham pleads for Sodom.**
Read Genesis 18. Here we read how the LORD and two angels appear to
Abraham as three men, and are given generous hospitality by him.

*Note: Abraham's nephew Lot and his family lived in Sodom although Abraham's
concern is for more than his own family.*

a) In verse 17 we have a glimpse into God's mind. What does it show about
God's assessment of Abraham? Would he ever say the same thing about us?

b) How would you describe Abraham's attitude to the LORD here? What are
Abraham's motives for the prayer? Do you think he is too bold?

c) How would you describe Abraham's pleading? "Carrying out negotiations",
"haggling" or "exploring the possibilities" with God?

d) The previous six chapters of the Bible tell of God's dealings with Abraham
over the previous quarter of a century. Do you think this has had an effect
on how Abraham prays?

e) Look at Isaiah 41:8–9: "But as for you, Israel my servant, Jacob my chosen
one, descended from my friend Abraham, I have called you back from the ends
of the earth so you can serve me. For I have chosen you and will not throw you
away." What title is Abraham given? What implications does this have for
praying? Is "God's friend" a title that we would like for ourselves? *(Note: The
idea of being a friend of God is pursued further in John 15:13–15.)*

f) Thinking about both Abraham here and Elijah on Mount Carmel, what
lessons can we learn about praying? ❑

Part 3) Prayer as relationship

◉ **Read Matthew 7:7–11.**

a) What three actions are encouraged here? What point is Jesus making about
prayer in order to reassure the disciples?
 The image of God as "Father" is used here and also three times in Matthew
6:5–8. We will look at this more in the next study. Here though, three
preliminary questions are important.

b) In a perfect world what would the characteristics of a father be? By using the
term "Father", what characteristics is Jesus implying that God possesses? The
passages of Matthew 6:6–8 and 7:7–11 are helpful here.

c) For those of us who have grown up in a Christian or "formerly Christian" culture, the idea that God is a "heavenly Father" is a concept that we take for granted. To get some idea of how radical it is, think through the following situations:

- Imagine you believe that God is an impersonal force or power (like electricity or gravity) that drives the universe.
  o How would you pray?
  Now imagine that you come to follow Jesus and his teaching.
  o What changes in your view of God would be most noticeable?
  o How would it affect the way you pray?
- Imagine you believe that God is a mighty, awesome judge, king, and ruler of the entire universe.
  o How would you pray?
  Now imagine that you come to follow Jesus and his teaching.
  o What changes in your view of God would be most noticeable?
  o How would it affect the way you pray?
- You believe that God is the great creator/designer who made everything but who now keeps his distance from the universe.
  o How would you pray?
  Now imagine that you come to follow Jesus and his teaching.
  o What changes in your view of God would be most noticeable?
  o How would it affect how you pray? ❏

Note: The use of the term "Father" for God can raise problems if we let our often negative or unsatisfactory experiences of our human fathers shape what we understand the word "Father" to mean. In looking at the Lord's Prayer we cannot avoid some discussion of God as father and at the start of the next study I have put a brief discussion of some of the issues involved. As part of the preparation for that study it would be helpful if all group participants could read that section in advance.

4) SUMMARY

Look again at Jesus' words "When you pray, don't babble on and on as people of other religions do. They think their prayers are answered only by repeating their words again and again. Don't be like them, because your Father knows exactly what you need even before you ask him! Pray like this..."

The fact that God is a living, personal God who is concerned about us dramatically affects how we pray.

a) What sort of God do the "babblers" think they are praying to? Do they know God as a person?

b) What is needed for communication between two people to take place? What is needed for such a communication to be maintained? How could that relationship be damaged?

c) The play-actors of the previous study ignored God and made the mistake of assuming that prayer was for their own benefit. The babblers of this study try to communicate with God but do so in the wrong way. What is the common link between these two wrong ways of praying?

d) Can we define prayer simply as "conversation with God"? Do we treat it like this? ❏

5) STEPPING OUT

Practical suggestions

- Do your prayers reflect the fact that God is a real, living, listening and caring God?
- When are you most tempted to "babble" in prayer? Why? What can you do to stop that tendency?
- Are we ever tempted to see God as someone who, if we offer him the right prayers, will give us what we want?
- Is the key to more effective praying knowing God better? How can we do that? ❏

Further study

If prayer is indeed communicating or conversing with God then it is linked with one of the great themes of the Bible: the relationship between God and humanity. Genesis 2 and 3 show how originally humanity had unbroken relations with God. A result of the banishment from Eden (Genesis 3:22–24) was the separation from God's presence.

- The Old Testament prophets looked forward to the restoration of relations between God and humanity. See, for instance, Isaiah 60:18–20 and Ezekiel 48:35.
- In the New Testament it is plain that these hopes of restoration are to be fulfilled in Jesus. See Matthew 1:23, Matthew 28:20, John 1:14, John 1:18.
- The whole Bible looks forward to total restoration of God's relations with the human race in heaven. See Revelation 21:3. ❏

Questions to think about

- In prayer, what is the opposite of babbling?
- Do you ever forget that God is a real and living God? How can we remind ourselves who God is?
- Is real prayer the *cause* of us knowing God personally or the *result* of us knowing God personally?
- Are our worship services ever just "babbling" or do they reflect a real awareness of God's presence?
- How will prayer be different in heaven? ❏

6) SUPPLEMENTARY MATERIAL

◉ a) Read Jeremiah 9:23–24 .

* What according to this passage is the greatest thing in the world? Do we believe it? Do we *live* as if we believe it? ❏

◉ b) Read Hosea 6:6.

* To offer a burnt offering as a sacrifice was the most costly part of the Jewish faith. How here does God view it?
* As Christians we may sacrifice our time, money or careers for God. But is this enough? ❏

c) Read Galatians 4:8–11.

* What characterized the Galatians' old faith?
* What changed when they became Christians? How, in verses 8 and 9, does Paul describe their new faith?
* How do you imagine their prayers changed after conversion?
* What futile things do people do today to try and find favour with God? ❏

STUDY 3

Privilege 1:
Praying to our Father...

"Our **Father** in heaven.... (Matthew 6:9a [NLT])

INTRODUCTION

The previous studies should have established two things. First, that true prayer *is not* a ritual to impress others, and second, that true prayer *is* a genuine and real communication between us and a personal, living, caring God.

With that in mind, it is now time to move on to the Lord's Prayer itself.

This is the first of two studies on the opening phrase of the Lord's Prayer, *Our Father in heaven*. In this study we will want to concentrate on one of the most remarkable and distinctive features of the teaching of Jesus and of his followers; the claim that God can be known as *Father*. In the next study we will look at the two other parts of this opening phrase; the word *Our* which is very significant and the concept that God is our Father *in Heaven*.

Note: The problem of God as Father.
Some people, because they have suffered at the hands of abusive fathers, find that to use the word "Father" for God raises all the wrong sort of associations. If this is a problem for you, then I sympathize. Throughout this study, I have tried to put forward alternatives to try and help people who find this a problem. As I suggested in the last study, it may be of some help to understand that God never says, "I am just like your father." Rather God himself defines fatherhood—he is the original, perfect, ideal Father and the Bible describes the characteristics of love and faithfulness that make up that fatherhood. It is inadequate human fathers that have devalued the idea of fatherhood, not God. All human fathers fall short of God's standard; some tragically so. For those that are hurting in this area to think about God as a "perfect parent" or "Abba" may be helpful. If this is a problem for you then you may find that it is best if you can talk privately to a trained counsellor about this. The truth that God loves us is so great that it is worth working towards being able to appreciate it.

Leader's Note: People who have had serious problems with their fathers are sadly widespread today and careless comments about it being "so wonderful that God is just like a father" can cause much distress. The wise leader will be aware of the issues raised above, be sensitive to feelings within the group and be ready to move things on when there is the danger of someone being hurt. The possibility that at least one person in a study group will need to talk privately to a minister or counsellor is something that must be borne in mind. While group Bible studies are of the greatest value, they are not normally the ideal setting for the discussion of deep felt and personal hurts. Issues like this, especially if they have involved abuse of any sort, are almost certainly something that should be worked out on a confidential basis with a minister or counsellor.

1) STARTER

Discuss *some* of the following:

- Has anyone ever agonized about how to address a letter?
- Has anyone ever been in a situation where they have had to address someone formally at work or professionally but been on first-name terms elsewhere?
- Think of either your mother or father. If someone were to ask you to list three ways in which you are like them and three ways in which you are unlike them, what would you say?
- If a computer could be programmed to find a pet animal that was most like your personality what would it come up with?

2) SURGERY

Discuss *some* of the following:

- What characteristics do you have that: a) you would wish to pass on to the next generation? b) you rather hope will die out with you?
- Who was the biggest influence on your life?
- If you were to imagine a drama sketch to show how you pray, which of the following would you be most like:
  o A slave bowing before their master.
  o A pupil being interviewed by an angry head teacher.
  o A criminal before a judge.
  o A subject standing before the Queen.
  o A conversation between friends in a café.
  o A child sitting next to its mum or dad.

o   A talkative and loud grandchild on the phone to its slightly dotty
grandparent.

3) STUDY

This is divided into two parts based on the Old and New Testament teaching.

Part 1) Old Testament

The idea of God as Father/Parent is present, but not fully developed, in the Old
Testament.

◉ **Have different people read out the following Bible verses** and as a group
decide *for each of them* what characteristic of God as parent they reveal:

* **Deuteronomy 1:29–31**
* **Deuteronomy 32:6**
* **Psalm 91:3–4**
* **Psalm 27:10**
* **Psalm 68:5**
* **Psalm 103:13**
* **Proverbs 3:12**
* **Isaiah 49:14–16**
* **Isaiah 63:16**
* **Isaiah 64:8**
* **Hosea 11:1–4**
* **Malachi 2:10**

Now discuss the following:

* What images seem to be strongest?
* Is the imagery exclusively male? Are they images of fathering, or
  parenthood in specific?
* Normally we let our images of earthly fathers define what God the Father
  is like. Supposing we turned it around: what do we learn about what a
  father should be like from the way God is Father?

Note: The problem of God as masculine

*A second problem with the image of God as Father is that some people feel that to use
the term father for God (along with talking about God as he) is to perpetuate a male-
dominated view of God. Let me make four points:*

* *To use the term "father" for God is to use an image to attempt to describe the
  indescribable. In reality, God is above gender.*
* *Christianity believes that to call God "Father" is not the result of a male-oriented
  culture describing God, but a term that God has revealed as being one that can be
  used of himself.*
* *Jesus not only knew God better than we do but was someone who was sympathetic*

to women and who frequently went against his own male-oriented culture. If there was a better term for God than "Father", we may be sure he would have used it.

- Although God never describes himself being a mother or wife (possibly because Israel was always tempted to follow the fertility gods of the neighbouring nations) he nevertheless uses female imagery of himself. In addition to the verses above, we see that in Isaiah (42:14; 46:3) God compares himself to a pregnant mother, in Psalm 22:9–10 God uses the image of a midwife for himself, and in Psalm 123:2 God likens himself to the mistress of a household. In Matthew 23:37 Jesus uses the image of a protective mother hen for himself!

Part 2) New Testament

a) Although the idea of God as "Father" was known in Jesus' time it seems to have been more as a theoretical concept than as a title to address God in prayer. Jesus however regularly talked about God as Father; there are over a hundred references in John's Gospel alone to God as Father. Let's look at four specific instances of Jesus praying.

◉ **Now have the following verses read in turn:**

- **Mark 14:36**   *Note: In this passage Mark preserves the original Aramaic* Abba, *the word a child would use for their earthly father. Using this word to talk to God seems to have been something that was distinctive of Jesus' way of praying.*
- **Matthew 11:25–26**
- **John 17:1–2**
- **John 17:25–26**   *Note: In the prayer of Jesus recorded in John 17 he calls God* "Father" *six times.*

- It is not enough to say that Jesus "knew God as his father" because there are many different attitudes sons can have to their fathers (fearful, trusting, disrespectful, etc.). Looking at these passages, how would you describe the sort of relationship to the Father that Jesus had?   ❏

b) A great deal of light is thrown onto both how Jesus viewed the idea of father and how God is like a father by the well-known parable in Luke 15. The "parable of the prodigal son", as it is traditionally called, reveals a great deal about how God the Father feels towards his children. We also need to bear in mind that in this story there are two lost sons.

Read Luke 15:11–32.

Note: The background to this story is that, in the land arrangements of the day, the younger son would have inherited about a third of the estate. In theory, he could have taken possession of it while his father was alive but the father would still have retained the income from it as long as he lived.

- By leaving (and presumably selling off his part of the estate) how has the son treated the father? Note the response of the elder son in verses 28–29.

- What do you imagine would be the appropriate response in this culture (or any other) to a son who did this to his father?
- In verses 21–24 what do we learn about the father's *attitude* and *actions* towards the younger son?
- This is the last of the three parables in Luke 15 about things being lost and then found and the introduction to all three is Luke 15:1–2. With that in mind what is the point that Jesus is making about God in this parable? How does it clarify what it means for God to allow himself to be called "*Father*"? ❑

◉ c) The relationship between Jesus and the Father is something that lies at the very heart of the Christian faith.

Read John 14:6–11.

- What, according to Jesus, is the relationship between him and the Father?
- How do we come to know the Father?
- What does this mean for those of us today who cannot now see Jesus physically (see v.9)?

Now have the following verses read in turn:

- **Romans 15:6**
- **2 Corinthians 1:3**
- **2 Corinthians 11:31**
- **Ephesians 1:3**
- **Colossians 1:3**
- **1 Peter 1:3**

- What title is given to God in every case? How does this link with the requirement given in John 14:6? Can we ever know God as "Father" apart from Jesus Christ? ❑

d) The fact that Jesus regularly and consistently used the term *Abba* of God was something that was so distinctive and precious that, over twenty years after his crucifixion and resurrection, Christians who spoke no Aramaic were regularly using the word.

Look at two passages together:

- **Romans 8:14–17**
- **Galatians 4:6–7**

Note: As the footnotes in The New Living Translation *indicate, the original Greek of both passages includes a reference to "Abba, Father".*

- In both passages what term is used to describe the status of those who are not Christians? What term is used to describe the status of Christians? What is the significance of this change of status?
- Both passages contain references to the Holy Spirit, and Romans 8:15 literally refers to "a spirit of adoption". What does this tell us about the work of the Holy Spirit?
- What do we learn from both passages about the results of being God's children? ❏

4) SUMMARY

a) Think about what your relationship to God is. If we take the Romans 8:14–17, Galatians 4:6–7 and John 14:6 passages we have just studied together what do we learn about the conditions that we have to meet before we know God as Father? Can you call God "Father"?

b) One of Jesus' disciples, the Apostle John, wrote perhaps the best summary of what it means to know God as Father. "See how very much our heavenly Father loves us, for he allows us to be called his children, and we really are!" (1 John 3:1).

- Does this truth encourage us?
- Do our lives reflect this truth?
- Does our praise reflect this truth?
- Do our prayers reflect this truth? ❏

5) STEPPING OUT

Practical suggestions
- What have you learned about God that can help you in your praying?
- Does knowing that God is our Father give us confidence in praying? Does it guarantee that all our prayers will be answered? So what *does* it guarantee? (See Matthew 26:39.)
- If you have become adopted into God's family then what relationship do you have to other Christians? What are the practical implications of this (Study 4 covers this further)?
- What is your biggest fear? How can the idea that God is your Father help you face it?
- If God is our Father and we are his sons and daughters then surely we ought to "bear the family resemblance". Do we? Is acquiring a better resemblance to God something that is an absolute priority for us? What can we do this week to bear more of a resemblance to our heavenly Father?
- The Apostle Paul applied the language of fatherhood to some of his relationships (i.e. 1 Timothy 1:2; Titus 1:4; 1 Thessalonians 2:11). How might we do the same in our churches? How would this build up the church? ❏

The following Bible passages may help us see how the Bible sees the role of a father.

i) **Fathers teach their children about God:** See Deuteronomy 6:4–9, 32:7; see also Psalms 44:1; 78:1–3 (where "ancestors" is literally, "fathers").

ii) **Fathers pray for their children:** See Job 1:5.

iii) **Fathers care for their children's well-being:** See Matthew 17:14–18; Luke 8:40–42; 49–56; John 4:43–54. ❏

Questions to think about

- Imagine you are talking about God to someone who has suffered under an oppressive, brutal, unloving or absent father and to whom the very word "father" is a complete turn-off. Could you explain the character of God to them without actually using the word father?
- Obviously many people today find problems with having God as a heavenly Father when their earthly father has been a source of hurt to them. Is there also a problem where the father has been too easy-going?
- What is the difference between a childish faith and a child-like faith?
- What are the dangers (if any) of over-emphasizing the concept of God as Father? How do we maintain a balance?
- You hear a preacher who, clearly avoiding any reference to God as Father, talks instead about God as "Parent". Is this a surrender to feminism and political correctness? Or is it a sensitive attempt to depict what God the Father stands for?
- What would you say to someone who, while rejecting the church, liked to pray to God as Father? ❏

6) SUPPLEMENTARY MATERIAL

a) In Romans 8 Paul touches on the future of the children of God.

Read Romans 8:14–25.

- What is the relationship between the Spirit of God and our being God's children? (See vv. 14, 16).
- What does this passage tell us about the future state of God's children? How does that give you hope?
- How does this passage encourage you to look forward to "that future day" when Christ is revealed with glory? (See vv. 19, 23).
- How does this passage encourage you to pray for those people who aren't members of God's family? ❏

b) Some of the key verses on the relationship between the Father and the Son are as follows:

- **Psalm** 2:7
- **Matthew** 3:16,17
- John 5:20
- John 6:44
- John 6:46
- John 10:30
- John 10:38
- John 14:10–11
- John 14:21

- On the basis of these verses what could we say about the relationship between Jesus and God the Father? ❏

c) **Ephesians 3:14–21** is a helpful passage on the significance of God as our Father.

Note: There is a pun in verse 14 that cannot be translated into English. In the Greek, Paul says he prays to the Father (pater) *from whom every* patria *(family, lineage or group) derives its name. The sense appears to be that of* The New Living Translation: *God is the father of all things and all people.*

- In this passage Paul is talking mainly about the wisdom, power and resources of God. Why do you think that he uses the title "Father" for God here?
- Paul obviously has lots of trust in God's resources—how does that show itself in what he prays?
- How do the things that Paul prays for give a picture of what he believes the Father to be like?
- What is the Father concerned about providing for his children?
- What is at the centre of the prayer in verses 17–19? How can this help us to be filled to the measure of all the fullness of God?
- Who could you pray this prayer for? Pray for them by inserting their name into the verses. ❏

STUDY 4

Privilege 2: Having a heavenly Father and an earthly family

"**Our Father** in heaven.... " (Matthew 6:9a [NLT])

INTRODUCTION

The previous study looked at the very important concept that underlies the whole of the Lord's Prayer: God wants to be known by his people as "Father". This study looks at two other vital things that come out of this first sentence of the Lord's Prayer: God is in heaven and he is not just *my* Father, he is *our* Father.

Leader's note: In this study I have put two separate—but linked—topics, "a heavenly Father" and "an earthly family" together.

---

1) STARTER

Discuss *some* of the following:

a) Read out the following advertising phrases. What comes to mind when you think of the following?

* The Chocolate Heaven Shop.
* The Rugby Heaven Website.
* The Shopping Heaven Experience.
* The Seafood Heaven Restaurant.
* Heavenly Holidays.

b) Which of the following do you expect to find in heaven?

* Angels with harps
* People sitting on clouds
* Dogs
* Elvis

c) What is the most close-knit community you have ever been in?

* Ante-natal class
* Army unit
* Teenage gang
* Football team

Why were you so close?

d) Which do you prefer:

- A deserted beach or one full of people?
- A half-empty café or one bustling with life?
- A quiet night in with a good book (or video), or a noisy party?

e) At home, what item or facility (car, computer, TV, bathroom, etc.) do you have to share that you really wish you had of your own?

f) What television family is the one that you most identify with? Which is the one that you would like to belong to? Why? ❏

2) SURGERY

Discuss *some* of the following:

- How would you answer the question, "Where is God now?"
- How do you imagine heaven? What sounds best about it to you?
- When, if ever, do you think about heaven? At funerals? When reading obituaries?
- Which is your church most like: A smoothly run business? A loving family? A dysfunctional family?
- If an artist was going to paint a portrait of you, what setting would he or she put you in?
- In what place do you say to yourself, "I really belong here?"
- Have you ever walked into a service at a church where you have never been before and suddenly felt really at home?
- When you pray, how much of your time is devoted to personal issues? How much is devoted to those issues that affect only other people?
- Say the following version of the Lord's Prayer aloud:

> My Father in heaven,
> may your name be honoured.
> May your kingdom come soon.
> May your will be done here on earth,
> just as it is in heaven.
> Give me my food for today,
> and forgive me my sins,
> just as I have forgiven those who have sinned against me.
> And don't let me yield to temptation,
> but deliver me from the evil one.
> For yours is the kingdom, the power and the glory.

- o How do you feel about saying this?
- o How has the significance of the prayer been altered? ❏

3) STUDY

This is divided into two parts: Part 1 deals with what it means for God to be our Father *in heaven*, and Part 2 deals with what it means for us to call God *our* Father.

Part 1) Our heavenly Father

The previous study concentrated on God as Father; this study deals with what it means for God to be a father who is *in heaven*.

At the outset, it is important to note that the Bible's view of heaven is very different from that of most people and even many Christians.

Leader's note: Although they may not emerge in the study there are several translation points with the word "heaven" that you ought to be aware of.

a) In English, although we say things like "the heavens opened" we normally distinguish between "heaven" and "the sky". However, in the biblical languages of Greek and Hebrew and in many other languages (e.g. French, *la ciel*), the same word is used for heaven and sky. Thus sometimes translators have to make a decision about whether to use "heaven" or "sky" (e.g. compare versions of Acts 1:10–11).

b) There appears to be little significant difference between *heaven* and *heavens*.

c) *Heaven* is sometimes used as an indirect way of referring to God as in Luke 15:18,21. For example, Matthew almost always refers to the "kingdom of heaven" rather than the "kingdom of God" (compare Matthew 4:17; Mark 1:15).

◉ a) The following verses are some of the many Bible passages that teach about heaven. They are listed in the order they appear in the Bible, rather than according to the aspect of heaven that they cover. Share them out among the group and have them read out one by one. After each is read out, discuss *very briefly* what it tells us about heaven. At the end of these verses I have put some summary questions.

- Genesis 1:1
- 1 Kings 22:19
- Nehemiah 9:6
- Psalm 103:19
- Isaiah 40:21–26
- Isaiah 63:15
- Isaiah 65:17
- Isaiah 66:1–2

- **Matthew 3:17**
- **Mark 13:32**
- Acts 7:54–56
- **Revelation 21:1–2**

To summarize:

In answering the following questions concentrate on what the texts you have read, rather than on any existing mental images that you have.

- Where did heaven come from?
- Who are the occupants of heaven?
- What are the characteristics of heaven?
- What will happen to heaven? ❑

◉ b) Although the book of Revelation is often thought of as dealing with the future it also shows us, in symbolic language, the invisible realities that lie behind the world around us. **Revelation 4:1–11** is a good example of this. As this chapter is read out, try to get the overall impression of what John feels and sees in his vision and try to avoid getting bogged down in the details of the imagery.

- Who is the central figure in the vision?
- What is the chief activity in heaven? What is its focus?
- If you were there how do you imagine you would feel?
- What we read about in this passage is actually occurring in heaven at this moment. If we could be more aware of this how would it change our lives? ❑

c) Read 2 Kings 6:8–23.

- Can you identify with the fears of Elisha's servant in verse 15?
- If you had been the servant, how would you have responded to Elisha's confident statement that "there are more on our side than on theirs"?
- What do we learn about the nature of heaven from this passage?
- Do we need to have our eyes opened to see the heavenly side of things? When do you need to see heaven's "horses and chariots of fire"? ❑

Part 2) Our earthly family

One of the great themes of the Bible is how God doesn't just save individuals; he makes himself a holy people. In the Old Testament this is the nation of Israel. In the New Testament, through the work of Jesus, God's people are not just a particular nation, they are a universal family.

◉ a) Have the following passages shared out and read.

- **Genesis 17:1–8**
- **Deuteronomy 27:9**

- How in the Old Testament times did someone become a member of God's people?
- What did God promise to his people?[1]
- What did God expect of his people in return?

◉ b) The New Testament continues the theme of God choosing a people. **Look at the following passages and answer the questions.**

i) **Matthew 12:48–50**

- What does Jesus say here is the condition of becoming his "brother, sister or mother"?
- What does he imply about the significance of natural family relationships?

ii) **Galatians 3:29**
    1 Peter 2:9–12
    2 Corinthians 6:18[2]
    Ephesians 2:19

- How are God's people defined now?
- Most of the original hearers of these letters would have been Christians who had been converted from a non-Jewish background. What do Paul and Peter say about the relationship of these people to the Old Testament people of God? What is the significance for us today?

iii) **Read the following: Galatians 6:10.** *(Note: the Greek literally here is "to the household [or family] of faith"),* **1 Timothy 5:1–2 Hebrews 10:24–25.**

- What do these passages tell us about the way we should relate to other believers in Christ?   ❑

---

1 Try not to become bogged down in the issue of the "Land of Canaan" or you will almost certainly find yourself generating more heat than light over modern Middle East politics. Most Christians have assumed that Christ fulfils this promise in that everything the land was to the Old Testament Jew (security, riches, blessing and peace, etc.) Jesus is (and much more) for the Christian.

2 This is a modification of 2 Samuel 7:14—"I will be his father, and he will be my son." It might be tempting to assume that the modification of the quotation to a plural and gender-inclusive form is the result of some politically correct modern translator. In fact, the changes are the Apostle Paul's!

4) SUMMARY

a) A heavenly Father

- In the Bible the presence of God the Father through Jesus Christ seems to be the main feature of heaven. Is it for us?
- How should the fact that God is in heaven affect our prayers when: a) we praise him? b) we confess our sins to him? c) we make requests to him?

b) An earthly family

- Like the word *"father"* (but to a lesser extent), the word *"family"* has also been devalued in modern society. Has our experience of modern dysfunctional, squabbling and fragmented human families given us too low a level of expectation about how our churches should be families?
- Becoming a Christian involves what we can call a *vertical* relationship to God; but it should also involve building what we can call *lateral* relationships with other Christians. Because there is a high level of individualism in modern Western culture, we can tend to neglect the lateral dimension. How can you improve your relationships with other Christians? ❑

5) STEPPING OUT

Practical suggestions

- How can we practise the art of seeing things from heaven's perspective?
- Why do we tend to think more of the idea of heaven during bad times in our life than during good times?
- Can you ever be "too heavenly minded to be of any earthly good"?
- Think of those people in the church who you find most difficult to get on with; does seeing them as "family" help?
- Is meeting together once or twice on Sunday (and perhaps shaking hands or nodding to each other) an appropriate way of expressing the fact that we are eternal brothers and sisters created by the death and resurrection of God's Son? How practically might we relate better to other Christians? ❑

Further study

i) Our heavenly Father

- **Genesis 28:10–17** is a helpful passage both about heaven and the nature of God's people.
- How Jesus thought of heaven and his own relationship to it are a profitable area for further study. There are ten references to heaven in **John 6:32–63** and from them we see how Jesus saw himself as the one who had come down from heaven as "the bread of life" and who would return to heaven. In **Acts 1:1–2** we have a reference to the return of Jesus to heaven. Jesus' position in heaven is referred to in **Acts 7:54–56**. **Hebrews 1:3** also refers to this. ❑

ii) Our earthly family

In **Ephesians 2:14–16** we have an important reference to the way that Jesus has united his followers together from whatever background they may have come.

There are many illustrations in the New Testament of the fact that believers are not just individuals but are bound together as part of the body of God's people which is itself linked into Christ. **John 15:1–7** uses the image of a spreading vine to make this point. **Romans 12:4–5** is one of a number of passages in the New Testament that talks about individual believers taking on the role of parts of a body. **1 Corinthians 12:12,27** uses similar images.

In **1 Peter 2:4–5**, the Apostle Peter offers another, less organic, image of how individual believers fit into the church; he sees Christians as individual stones making up a spiritual building. ❏

Questions to think about

- You are talking to a science-fiction fan about heaven. They ask whether heaven is another dimension. Do you agree?
- Do attempts by artists to depict heaven visually help or hinder our understanding of what heaven is like?
- It has been alleged that the Christian view of heaven numbs the desire to do good in this life. Should this be the case?
- As a Christian do you think of yourself as being an individual or as being part of a family? The dangers of being a lone Christian are fairly obvious but are there problems with seeing yourself only as part of a church?
- When we sin does that just affect us personally or does it also affect our church?
- Imagine two people in the first century: a Jew devoted to keeping the laws on purification who can trace his ancestry back to Abraham, and a pagan who has worshipped some of the wildest and weirdest idols around. Both become Christians. How would you imagine the Jew would react to being told that he was now a brother of the former pagan and that this man too had now inherited the promise to Abraham?
- What would you say to someone who said, "I want to follow Jesus but I can't stand the idea of being forced to be nice to other Christians"? ❏

6) SUPPLEMENTARY MATERIAL

a) One person in the Old Testament who, at least in the early part of his life, was well aware of the nature and reality of heaven was Solomon. In 1 Kings 8 we read of his great prayer at the dedication of the temple. **Read 1 Kings 8:22–54.**

- What attitude to God do you detect here?
- There must have been a temptation for Israelites to imagine that the LORD lived in the temple. How does Solomon's prayer go against that belief?
- Solomon repeatedly points out that God is in heaven. Do you feel that this emphasis on heaven makes him think that God is remote from the world?

- Are we inclined to think of God as being localized somewhere (church?) Or do we see him as being too far away to care? ❏

b) Although Christians often talk about dying as "going to heaven" this is not the emphasis of the Bible. **Read 2 Corinthians 5:8; Philippians 1:21–23; 1 Thessalonians 5:10.**

How is death seen here for the believer? What is the focus of the hope?

- Is this aspect of death central in our thinking? ❏

STUDY 5

Praise: Honouring God's name as holy

"May your name be honoured." (Matthew 6:9b [NLT])

INTRODUCTION

We have now moved to the first of the petitions of the Lord's Prayer; that God's name be honoured or hallowed. Jesus here sets out the right priority for all praying; our prayers should first of all start with God and with praising God.

1) STARTER

Either do the following exercise *or* discuss some of the questions below.

Exercise

Flood waters (or a fire) are sweeping towards your house! The police have given you five minutes to salvage what is valuable and put it in a single holdall. What would you grab?

Questions

- You are at the dentist and in the course of a nasty bit of drilling the dentist tells you to "think of something pleasant". What does your mind turn to?
- Who do you consider as someone who has not been treated fairly by public opinion? You might think of some actor, artist, sportsperson or politician. Why do you think that their lack of fame or reward is unfair?
- Where have you seen someone do something that you felt was remarkably selfish?
- *Either* What advertisements or TV programmes have annoyed you recently by caricaturing a person, an institution or something you respect? *Or* How would you feel if someone made a vicious verbal attack on your home town?
- *Either* Has anybody got a name that means something? Has its meaning affected how you live? *Or* Have you ever wanted to change your name? Why?
- Who has ever bought something on the basis of the product "having a good name" but been disappointed? How did you feel?
- Who has ever been given a personal promise or guarantee by someone important?
- Who has ever been dangerously close to something (e.g. a live 20,000-volt cable, a 200-foot cliff edge, a deadly animal?) What sensations did you feel?

- Who has ever been in a situation where you were glad that no one around knew you were a Christian? ❏

2) SURGERY

Discuss some of the following.

- It has been argued that a crude but effective indicator of what a society worships can be found by seeing what sort of magazines people read. Imagine an alien adopting such a viewpoint and going to your biggest local newsagent. On this basis, what would it conclude about what was worshipped in your community?
- Another indicator of what is an idol is more subtle: an idol is "something that people sacrifice things to". What instances of this can you think of?
- If you went out into your local shopping centre and asked people what came into their heads when they heard the word "holy" what do you think they would say? Why?
- In how many different ways (good and bad) is God's name used in everyday life today? ❏

3) STUDY

This is divided into two parts. Part 1 looks at what "God's name" means and Part 2 examines what it means to "honour his name as holy".

Part 1) God's name

a) In the Bible a name was not just the identifying label that it tends to be in our culture, rather it meant something. People were conscious of the meaning of names and believed there was a connection between a name and the person who bore it. What according to your Bible footnotes is the meaning of the following names?

- Esau   Genesis 25:25
- Jacob   Genesis 25:26
- Moses   Exodus 20:10
- Jesus   Matthew 1:21   ❏

◉ b) In the case of God there is a very strong connection between his name and the reality it represents. **Read Exodus 3:14–15**, paying attention to any footnotes.

If the meaning of God's name here is "I Am the One Who Always Is" or "I am", what is that saying about him? In the context of making promises or covenants to his people why would a name with such a meaning have a special significance?

- If the name "the LORD/ Yahweh" (see Leader's Notes below) was the name guaranteeing God's covenant promises to his people then why would it be important for them to respect it?

- In the New Testament Jesus uses the expression "I am" of himself in a remarkable way. **Read John 8:54–59** (in the NLT you should note the footnote to verse 58). What evidence do you see that Jesus' use of expression "before Abraham was I am" is understood as a claim that he is God (see Leviticus 24:16)?
  Note: There are seven other declarations of Jesus in John's Gospel with an emphatic "I am" which seem to refer to the name of God; they are listed in the Further study *part of the STEPPING OUT section.*

Leader's note: The most common word in the Bible is the four Hebrew consonants *yhwh* which represents the Old Testament name of God. In Hebrew, the vowels in the Bible were not written down until quite late in Jewish history, by which time it had been decided that the name of God was too holy to pronounce. The result is that we do not know for certain what the name sounded like. It is now assumed that it was probably pronounced Yahweh. The name is related to the announcement in Exodus 3:14 that God is "I AM THE ONE WHO ALWAYS IS" and in it God defines himself as "I am". In English Bibles it is traditional to use "the LORD" to represent *yhwh*. Two things are important: a) The LORD is not a title (as in Lord Nelson) but a unique personal name. b) For Christians *yhwh* has been replaced as the covenant name for God by "Father" or "Jesus".

---

c) The Bible frequently talks about the "name of the Lord" and the "name of Jesus". **Read the following:**

- **Psalm 75:1.** Literally, as in NIV and other versions, this is "For your wondrous works declare that your name is near."
- **Psalm 91:14**
- **Acts 4:12** (Talking of Jesus)
- **Philippians 2:9** (Also talking of Jesus)

In these passages what is the link between the name and the person of God or Jesus?

- Why then are we: a) "not to misuse God's name" (Exodus 20:7)?
  b) "to honour God's name"? ❏

◉ d) Throughout the Old Testament God uses other names for himself, each of which reveal more of who he is. **Read at least some of the following verses in turn.** As each one is read, try to summarize briefly what the title means. Ask yourself which name on the following list rings true for you. Do you have a story that you can tell to the group of how God proved himself true to his name?

- **Genesis 22:14**   *Yahweh Yir'eh* (Jehovah Jireh) "The Lord Will Provide."
- **Exodus 15:26**   *Yahweh Rapheka* "The Lord who heals me."
- **Exodus 17:15**   *Yahweh Nissi* (Jehovah Nissi) "The Lord Is My Banner."
- **Judges 6:24**   *Yahweh Shalom* (Jehovah Shalom) "The Lord Is Peace."
- **1 Samuel 17:45** *Yahweh Tsebaoth* "The Lord Almighty" or "The Lord of Hosts." ❑

(Note: The idea here seems to be that God is the Lord of all heaven's angelic armies.)

- **Genesis 49:24**   *Shepherd*
- **Psalm 95:3**   *King*
- **Genesis 18:25**   *Judge*
- **Isaiah 44:24**   *Redeemer*
- **Exodus 15:3**   *Warrior*
- **Psalm 18:2**   *Rock*
- **Psalm 18:2**   *Fortress*
- **Isaiah 1:4**   *The Holy One*
- **Genesis 49:24**   *The Mighty One*
- **Daniel 7:9**   *Ancient of Days* ❑

(Note: Those titles that you have not looked at can be studied later.)

- Which of these names reveals a characteristic of God that you need to know, or be reminded of, in your own life at the present time?
- Which of these names reveal a characteristic of God that your church most needs to know, or be reminded of, at the present time? ❑

Part 2) Honour as holy

Older versions of the Lord's Prayer talk about "hallowing" God's name. Newer versions have a problem with this word, which means to "treat or respect as holy". The real difficulty is actually not the *word* "hallow", it is the *concept*; the entire idea of anything being holy has largely slipped from modern Western minds. We need to do some homework on holiness.

◉ **a) Read Isaiah 6:1–8.**
Isaiah's vision took place in the temple around 740 BC. It was the year that, after having ruled for over half a century, King Uzziah died. Although Uzziah started off being a good king at a very young age (you can read about him in 2 Chronicles 26) pride caused him to attempt to offer incense in the temple; something that only a priest could do. This led to Uzziah's judgement by God with leprosy and his enforced isolation.

- A fifty-two-year reign of relative stability and prosperity had ended; the head of the nation had gone to his grave as a man under God's displeasure; the international scene was troubled by the rise of the brutal Assyrian empire. What thoughts do you think might have been going through Isaiah's mind as he went to the temple?

- What, according to verses 1–4, did Isaiah see, hear, feel and smell in the temple? What impression would Isaiah have received from these sensations?
- What does the refrain in verse 3 say about God? Why do you think the word "holy" is repeated three times?
- Why does Isaiah despair of his life in verse 5? Would that have been your reaction? What aspect of his life appears to have troubled him the most?
- What happened on the altar as part of the temple ritual? What would being touched by a coal from the altar have signified to Isaiah?
- King Uzziah had died a feeble, powerless man who had been made ritually unclean by his sin. How is God different from Uzziah?
- Is the fact that God is holy something that you can fully explain or is it something that you have to experience?

(Note: It is interesting to compare this vision with that given to John in Revelation 4:1–11. You probably looked at this passage in the last study but is worth re-reading for the light it sheds on God's holiness.) ❑

b) Many of the Psalms praise God's holiness. **Psalm 99** is a good example. This psalm repeatedly affirms the LORD's holiness.

- What aspects of God's holiness are celebrated in verses 1–3?
- What aspects of God's holiness are praised in verse 4?
- Verses 6 and 7 list three great priests[3] of Israel's history. Why does the gap between a holy God and sinful human beings make a priesthood necessary? How does Jesus fulfil that role for Christians? (See Hebrews 2:17–18—"Therefore, it was necessary for Jesus to be in every respect like us, his brothers and sisters, so that he could be our merciful and faithful High Priest before God. He then could offer a sacrifice that would take away the sins of the people. [18] Since he himself has gone through suffering and temptation, he is able to help us when we are being tempted." And 7:26—"He is the kind of high priest we need because he is holy and blameless, unstained by sin." etc.)
- What aspects of God's holiness are praised in verses 8 and 9?
- Is God's holiness just a matter of his power and majesty? ❑

◉ c) The idea that God is holy has implications for how we live. **Read Exodus 19:5–6. Leviticus 11:44–45.**
If God is holy, how are his people to live?

- What did being holy or separate mean for the Old Testament Jew?
- What does it mean for the Christian today to be part of "a holy nation"? ❑

◉ d) The idea that God is holy has implications for how we pray. A generation after Isaiah's vision, in 701 BC, King Hezekiah of Judah faced a crisis when

---

3. Although not technically a priest, Moses was involved in the institution of the priesthood, acted himself as an intermediary between God and the people, and interceded for the people before the LORD.

Jerusalem was surrounded by the armies of the Assyrian ruler Sennacherib. Their generals send a demand to King Hezekiah for the surrender of the city. **Read Isaiah 37:1–20.**

- In a crisis like this would your priority have been the same as Hezekiah's?
- Hezekiah had close links with the prophet Isaiah (see Part 1). How does his prayer reflect a similar view of God's holiness? What sort of God does he believe in?
- Hezekiah's prayers were spectacularly answered (see Isaiah 37:36–38). Are you surprised?
- There were specific aspects to Hezekiah's situation that we do not share today; Hezekiah was the king of God's people and there were specific covenant promises that had been made that applied to his situation. Nevertheless how can we adopt a similar attitude in our prayers? ❏

4) SUMMARY

a) Think about God's name

- How big is your God? Do you feel that your mental image of God is large enough to do justice to who he actually is?
- How can we gain a richer and truer understanding of what God's name means or who God is? ❏

b) Think about how we honour God as being holy

- Why do you think honouring God's name comes first in the Lord's Prayer? ❏

c) Think about how we can live as people who honour God's name

- How can individual Christians dishonour God's name? How can churches dishonour God's name?
- When we think about praising or worshipping God do we simply think in terms of saying words and singing songs? What other ways of worship are there? Can we worship God by our work or leisure activities? ❏

5) STEPPING OUT

Practical suggestions

- Either privately or publicly take time to praise God for who he is. Give him thanks and honour him for who he is. That might mean singing or saying praises; it might mean doing something more creative like taking your favourite psalm and rewriting it into your own spoken English.
- One inevitable result of honouring God as holy is to recognize how far short we fall from his standards. As a result you might well feel that you need to spend some time privately confessing to God those things you have done that are wrong.
- Prayerfully examine your life. Does it reflect God's holy standards? Ask God to show you what you can do to be more holy. In what particular area of

your life do you think God would like to help you develop greater holiness? Pray for each other over this.

- Ask how you can bring honour to God at home, at work and in your community.
- **Read Philippians 4:4–9.** Resolve to aim to live this out next week.
- Make a conscious decision now that when you come into contact with someone who isn't speaking or living as if God's name was to be honoured as holy, that you will pray for them.

Further study

- Look at any of the names of God given in the study section that you did not discuss earlier and think about what they mean.
- There is much in the Old Testament about the danger of honouring God with our words but not with our lives. See for example:
  - Amos 5:21–24
  - Hosea 6:6
  - Isaiah 1:10–17
- In John's Gospel Jesus makes seven declarations with an emphatic "I am" which seem to refer to the name of God in Exodus 3:14 and which are related to Jesus' claim in John 8:54–59. These are as follows:
  - John 6:35
  - John 8:12; 9:5
  - John 10:7,9
  - John 10:11,14
  - John 11:25
  - John 14:6
  - John 15:1,5

  It is well worth exploring what these titles mean. To do this properly may require a good study Bible with cross-references or a good commentary on John's Gospel. How do these titles of Jesus apply to us in our daily lives? ❏

Questions to think about

- What would you say to a new Christian who came to you and told you that because they were called to be holy, they were going to separate themselves off from everyone and everything in the world that wasn't holy?
- How do you handle it when someone swears using the name of God or Jesus Christ?
- You are watching an amazing wildlife programme when someone says, "Isn't Nature wonderful!" How do you respond?
- How can a church honour God's name in a community?
- Which of the following would be ways that a Christian in the business world could honour God?
  - Hang a Bible text over their desk?
  - Pay their taxes?
  - Refuse to listen to dirty jokes?
  - Sell a good product for a fair price?

- o Forbid the misuse of Christ's name in their office?
- Is there a gap between our praise and our practice?   ❏

6) SUPPLEMENTARY MATERIAL

a) Jesus' own attitude to holiness is worth studying.

That Jesus himself was holy is something that he claimed both directly and indirectly. "Why do you call it blasphemy when the Holy One who was sent into the world by the Father says, 'I am the Son of God'?" John 10:36 "For them I sanctify myself, that they too may be truly sanctified" John 17:19 (NIV). The key words in this sentence to *sanctify* and be *sanctified* mean to "be made holy" or "separated". Jesus was also recognized as being holy, see John 6:68, Acts 2:27; 3:14 and 4:27,30.

But what does holiness mean? Many of Jesus contemporaries felt they knew what it meant to be holy. **Read Luke 5:33–35; 6:6–11; 7:36–39; 15:1–2.**

- On the basis of these verses what sort of life would you have had to lead to be known as a holy person according to the rules of the Jewish leaders? What actions would have marked your lifestyle?
- In what ways can we slip into the same trap that these religious leaders had fallen into?

Yet Jesus' understanding of holiness was very different. **Read Mark 7:1–23.**

- How does Jesus redefine holiness here?
- If holiness is not external rules, what is it? What does this mean about how we are to show and live holiness?
- How important is holiness? **Read Hebrews 12:14.**
- How are we to be holy? **Read 1 Thessalonians 3:12–13.**   ❏

b) What is the significance of the Holy Spirit in helping us to become holy? **Read 1 Corinthians 6:11 and Titus 3:5, 1 Corinthians 6:19, Galatians 5:16–17.**   ❏

Purpose: Knowing the meaning of life

"May your Kingdom come soon. May your will be done here on earth, just as it is in heaven." (Matthew 6:10 [NLT])

INTRODUCTION

We now move to the second of the petitions of the Lord's Prayer—that God's kingdom would come and that God's will would be done. Some people try to divide this petition into two: identifying one prayer for the coming of the kingdom and another for doing God's will. In reality it is hard to separate these; after all, when God's will is done, his kingdom spreads.

This clause of the Lord's Prayer goes to the heart of God's intentions and actions in his world. The idea of God as King, God's kingdom and the need for God's people to be loyal citizens under God's kingship are themes that are close to the heart of the Bible and are either directly or indirectly referred to on every one of its pages. This study concentrates on Jesus' teaching of the kingdom, with only the briefest outline of some of these other aspects.

1) STARTER

Either do the following exercise *or* discuss some of the questions below.

Exercise

Preparation: Have a large pile of old newspapers, colour supplements and popular magazines.

Go round the group assigning alternative people as "Hopes" and "Fears". Then, in twos (one "Hopes" and one "Fears") have them go through the papers etc for five minutes looking for images that sum up their hopes or fears (either for themselves or for the world). Then, in the last five minutes, go round the group getting people to display what they have found.   ❏

Questions
- What's the point of the church?
- Who do you know (or know of) who has built an empire? (You can define an empire however you want.)
- What do you rule over? Your firm, your bedroom, your desk, your garden?
- Do you like to rule or to be ruled?
- What images and emotions do the words "king" or "queen" conjure up for you? How might your distant ancestors have reacted differently to the same words?   ❏

2) SURGERY

Discuss some of the following:

- The nineteenth century American writer Henry Thoreau wrote that most people "lead lives of quiet desperation". Do you agree?
- If you were to come back to your present city, town or village in a hundred years what would you expect to see? A gleaming hi-tech city? A tranquil utopia? A polluted and derelict urban wasteland? A deserted, silent wilderness? Something else?
- In a single sentence how would you answer the question: what is the purpose of your life?
- Think of a king or queen during the Middle Ages (or earlier) with unchallenged power? What would people have expected them to do in order to be a "good monarch"? ❏

3) STUDY

This is divided into six topics. Try to consider each topic, however briefly.

a) The kingdom is God's dominion

◉ In his letter to the church at Colossae, Paul writes about what God has done for believers in Christ. **Read Colossians 1:13–14.**

- What kingdoms are described here? Who rules each kingdom?
- What was the original state of those who are now followers of Christ?
- What do we learn about how they switched kingdoms?

The kingdom of God was central to Jesus' ministry (see, for example, Mark 1:14–15, Matthew 4:23 and Acts 1:3).

What did Jesus mean by this? In the Old Testament the idea of God's kingdom was centred on the physical land of Israel and a human and visible king. Read out the following three passages, briefly noting the context of the conversation. After each one is read, ask what do we learn about the kingdom from this passage:

- John 18:33,36
- Luke 17:20–21
- Acts 1:6–8

◉ Now read **Luke 7:18–23** and **Luke 11:20.** What do these passages tell us about the signs by which the kingdom of God indicates its presence?

- It is easy to divide the universe into compartments. One is "spiritual" or "heavenly" and the other is "physical" or "worldly". Where does the kingdom of God fit into this idea? Or is the whole idea of compartments a fallacy? ❏

b) The kingdom of God is dynamic

The nature of the kingdom of God is illustrated in a number of Jesus' parables.

◉ Read Mark 4:26–29.

- What is the farmer's role in making the wheat grow?
- What aspects of its growth does the farmer have no control over?
- Is this an invitation to be spiritually lazy and "let God do it all"?

Read Matthew 13:31–32. Although exactly which plant Jesus was referring to here is unclear, the principle is plain: "great oaks from little acorns grow".

- How does this rule apply to the kingdom?
- Give an example of the sort of "small seed" that may start a work of the kingdom.
- Give an example of the sort of "large plant" that might result.
- Give an illustration of a discouraging situation where this teaching might be helpful.

Both Jesus and Paul talk about the kingdom as having come and yet also being something that is still to come. How does the idea that the kingdom is the dynamic and growing rule of God help explain this?　❑

c) The kingdom of God is a delight

The word associated with Jesus' preaching is the *gospel*, literally "the good news".

Read Luke 8:1.

- What is the best "good news" that you have ever had to announce?
- Is the description "good news" one that might be used to describe how you talk about Jesus? If not, why?

The imagery Jesus used of the kingdom of God is very striking.

◉ Read the following: Matthew 22:1–4 and Luke 14:15–16.

- According to Jesus what characterises the kingdom of God?
- When non-Christians think of Christianity do they think of it as being "good news"? If not, why not?
- If we had more experience of the kingdom as being a delight, would sharing Jesus with others be any easier?　❑

d) The kingdom of God is divisive

Although the kingdom is a delight, we are also reminded that there is something divisive about it. We learn in the Gospels that not everybody enters the kingdom.

◉ Go round the group allocating to an adjacent pair of people one of the following stories that Jesus told. Have them glance through the story and decide which are the two contrasting elements or images within it.

- **Matthew 13:47–48**
- **Luke 3:17**
- **Matthew 13:24–30**
- **Matthew 25:1–13**
- **Matthew 25:14–30**

> o Go round the group asking for the contrasting pairs. What does the absence of a middle way between the two opposing images suggest about the kingdom?
> o What picture do you get from these parables about the ultimate results of being in the kingdom? About the ultimate results of being out of the kingdom?
> o What lessons are there for us in this sharp division? ❑

e) The kingdom of God needs a decision
◉ Read Matthew 21:28–32.

- How do you imagine that someone who had the mindset of the older son would have responded to the offer of the kingdom? Someone with the younger son's outlook?
- What point is Jesus making here about how we approach the good news of the kingdom? Is it one that still needs to be made?

Read Luke 18:15–17.

- What do you think Jesus means here?
- How do we show child-like faith without being childish?

◉ Read Matthew 13:44–46.

- How would you update these parables to our modern business culture?
- What is Jesus saying here about making the decision to follow him and get into the kingdom? ❑

f) The kingdom makes demands
The privileges of being in the kingdom cannot be separated from the responsibilities. So, for example, Jesus warned his contemporaries about the danger of losing the privilege of being in the kingdom.

◉ Read Matthew 21:43.

- From this passage what is the relationship between being in the kingdom and doing good things?

Read Matthew 25:31–46.

- What title is given to Jesus here in verses 34 and 41?
- What does the fate of the sheep and the goats hinge on? Some people suggest that being in the kingdom is simply a "spiritual" matter. What does this passage suggest about what it means to be in the kingdom?
- How does this challenge you now?

◉ **Read the following passages from Paul's letters.**

- **Romans 14:17**
- **1 Corinthians 4:20**
- **1 Corinthians 5:9**
- **Galatians 5:19–21**

  From these passages what do we learn...
  - about what the kingdom of God *is*?
  - about what the kingdom of God *isn't*?
  - On the basis of these verses did Paul consider the kingdom to be something in the present, something in the future or something that was in both? ❏

4) SUMMARY

a) To pray for the kingdom of God to come implies that, at the moment, the rule or dominion of God has only partially come.

- How has the kingdom come so far...
  - in your life?
  - in your church fellowship?
  - in your community?
  - in the world?

- What would it mean for the kingdom to come more fully...
  - in your life?
  - in your church fellowship?
  - in your community?
  - in the world? ❏

b) The Bible teaches that one day the kingdom of God will suddenly come in all its fullness and power (see, for example, Matthew 24:3, 1 Corinthians 15:23, 1 Thessalonians 2:19).

- Briefly outline what the arrival of the Kingdom of God in all its fullness and power with Christ's return would mean: a) for the follower of Jesus b) for someone who had rejected Jesus?
- Does the kingdom of God give your life purpose? Is the kingdom the great priority by which you measure the goals of your life? ❏

5) STEPPING OUT

Practical suggestions

- Either privately or publicly take time to praise God for the extent that his kingdom has so far come in your life.
- Pray for the kingdom to come more fully in your own life, and among those you are in contact with.
- Ask yourself what you can practically do to help God's kingdom come more fully in your home, your place of work and your community.
- Do you have a burning desire for the kingdom to come in your community? Ask God to give you a greater desire for this. ❏

Further study

There are many themes to do with the kingdom of God that could be studied further. I have listed two below but the supplementary material covers another major theme. For each theme I have listed a few verses to look at; a Bible with cross-references would give you many more verses.

i) God the King and his kingdom

The Old Testament talks only in passing about God's kingdom; it does however talk a lot about God as King.

- Ask members of the group to read out the following passages in turn. After each one, summarize what it has told you about how God is king.
  - o Isaiah 6:5
  - o Isaiah 43:15
  - o Exodus 15:18
  - o 1 Chronicles 29:11

- In the previous study we looked at Psalm 99. This is one of a series of Psalms (numbers 93–99) that celebrate God's kingship. **Read Psalm 93.**
  - o What is the LORD king over?
  - o What do we learn about the nature of God's rule?
  - o From where does the LORD reign? (See also Psalm 99:1–2.)
  - o What do you feel is the mood of the psalm writer here? (See also Psalm 95:1–2 and 97:1.) ❏

ii) What does it mean to be a member of the kingdom of God?

Read the following passages:

- **Exodus 19:6**
- **1 Peter 2:9**
- **Revelation 1:6**
- **Ephesians 2:4–6**

- What is the significance of Jesus' followers being priests?
- What is the significance of them reigning with him in the heavenly realms?

Questions to think about

- If we take Jesus as Lord and king what are our duties to him? What are his responsibilities to us?
- What, at this moment in your life, is God's will for you? Are you seeking it? Doing it? Avoiding it? Is finding God's will for your life even an issue?
- Imagine that the following people have either decided to become Christians or desire to take their Christianity seriously. They want to work out the implications of the kingdom in their lives.
  - A teacher.
  - A newsagent.
  - An MP.
  - A police officer.
  - Someone who is engaged in the import/export business with the developing world.
  - An advertising executive for a cigarette company.

  What might they decide to do, or not to do, as a result of that decision?
- "If we pray 'may your kingdom come' we must be willing to pray 'may my kingdom go'." Where do our own little kingdoms come into conflict with God's kingdom? What should we do about it? What would help you to see God's kingdom more present in your own life?
- What is the difference between the church and the kingdom?
- Could a Christian political party ever have the slogan "Vote for us and make the kingdom come"?
- The picture that the Bible teaches is that our world is a place where there is a continuous and ongoing battle between the kingdoms of God and the devil. Is that how we perceive it? Should we think of the world this way?
- When we come face to face with evil in this world should we be realistic (the kingdom has not yet fully come) or optimistic (the kingdom is yet to come)?
- What is the relationship between mission and extending the kingdom of God?

6) SUPPLEMENTARY MATERIAL

A great theme in the Bible is how Jesus fulfils all the Old Testament promises about the coming king or Messiah. This is something that can only be briefly outlined here.

Background

The nation of Israel was ruled by kings from around 1050 until 586 BC. Only the second king, David, even remotely lived up to the duty to be God's representative on earth, and after him (as the Old Testament books of 1 and 2 Kings painfully relate) the monarchy slid into decline and division until God eliminated it. Although the human kingship of Israel was a failure, there came with it the idea that, one day, from the line of King David there would come the perfect king. In 2 Samuel 7 especially verses 12–16 we read how God established a solemn covenant with David that his dynasty would endure. This view is summarized in Psalm 89. **Read Psalm 89:1–4,29** which express this poetically.

- What is the promise here?
- Do you think it could be fulfilled by a purely human line of kings?
- Imagine that you are a Jew around the time of Jesus' birth. Six hundred years have passed since the last king. You are taxed, bullied and insulted by the occupying pagan Romans. How would you view these thousand-year-old promises to David?

Note: Many of the Old Testament psalms are addressed to the king. In some cases they seem to have several levels of meaning and to refer not only to the human king ruling on David's throne, but also to a supernatural or divine king (see for example Psalms 45,110).

There are many other prophecies of a coming king from the line of David in the Old Testament. Linked with this coming king are promises of the creation of a glorious rule that would far exceed anything possessed by David or his son Solomon. Part of the process of crowning a king involved anointing him with holy oil (see 2 Samuel 5:3 and Psalm 89:20). The word used for the anointed one was *masiah* which in Greek was either written down as *Messiah* or translated as *Christ*.

Three great passages from Isaiah expand on the vision of the king descended from David.

Read
- **Isaiah 2:1–5**
- **Isaiah 9:6**
- **Isaiah 11:1–12**

Leader's note: Christians debate about how literally these promises are to be taken. Don't get side tracked onto vegetarian lions (verse 7) or who "the remnant" are (verse 11).

From these passages.

- What do we learn about the Messiah?
- What do we learn about the nature of the Messiah's rule?
- What do we learn about the extent of the Messiah's kingdom?
- Is the one who is prophesied human or divine (note Isaiah 9:6 and 11:2)? ❏

In Daniel 7 we read how Daniel saw in a dream a series of terrifying visions of four beasts that symbolized future world empires. Finally he sees a new vision. **Read Daniel 7:9–14.**

- Who is the figure that dominates the vision in verses 9–10?
- What is his task? (vv. 9–12)? (Try to avoid getting tied up with the issues of specifically who the beasts represent.)
- What new figure is introduced in v. 13?
  NOTE: *Literally the figure in v.13 is described as being one like "a son of man". It is a term that Jesus frequently uses of himself in the Gospels.*
- What do we learn about the scope and duration of his kingdom? ❑

Provision: Asking for what God wants to give us

STUDY 7

"Give us our food for today." (Matthew 6:11 [NLT])

INTRODUCTION

We now come to the third petition of the Lord's Prayer: that we would be given food (literally, bread) for today. As we move into the second part of the Lord's Prayer the focus has shifted from us asking for God's name to be glorified and his kingdom, to asking God to meet our needs. The language is no longer "you" and "your", it is now "us" and "our". This part of the prayer is making our will conform to God's will. We are not just praying here for what we want; we are also praying that we will want what God wants for us.

To pray for food or bread is the most down-to-earth and practical request to make of God. Yet as we look at it we will see it is a request that raises many issues.

1) STARTER

Either do the following exercise *or* discuss some of the questions below.

Exercise

Do one of the following

a) Pick three everyday items out of the food cupboard—for example, a can of beans, a packet of pasta, a jar of jam, breakfast cereal, a chocolate bar, a tin of tuna, etc. As a group try to list:

i)   All the processes that this food has been through in order to bring it to your cupboard.
ii) The things that could stop it from appearing in your cupboard.   ❏

b) Imagine that you are the captain of a lifeboat adrift in the tropics with eight people in it and you are running out of food and water. You are drifting towards an inhabited island but it will be a week before you get there. The calculations on your supplies suggest that you have two options.

- Option A: select half the passengers and give them the food and water. This will guarantee the survival of these four people.
- Option B: you all share the food and water equally but the likelihood is that none of you will survive.

Which option do you choose and why? If you go for Option A how do you choose who is to get the supplies? ❑

c) Think of your grandparents when they were your age.
- What would have been their most valued possession?
- What would they have used for transport?
- How would they have communicated with distant friends?
- What would they have had to play music on?
- What would have been a luxury holiday for them?
- What would have been a luxury food for them?
- Would they have seen themselves as being impoverished? ❑

Questions
Discuss some of the following:

a) Have you ever been in a situation where you have wondered where your next meal was coming from? What happened? ❑

b) Imagine you could have a meal, anywhere in the world with any four famous people of your choice, alive or dead. Who would you choose? Where would you eat? What would you eat? ❑

c) Have you ever been on a monotonous diet? How did you feel about being able to switch back to something different? ❑

d) What is the absolute minimum amount of money per year that a family of four would need to survive in your area? What would be the minimum needed to live fairly well? *(Note: Be sensitive here to the possibility that there may be those in the group who live on a limited income.)* ❑

2) SURGERY
Discuss some of the following:

a) Consider the following statistics:

- The world's richest 225 individuals have a combined wealth equal to the annual income of the poorest 47% of the world's population (which passed the six-billion mark in 2000).
- According to UN figures, if the world's richest 200 people were to give up 1% of their wealth each year, they could pay for every child on Earth to have free access to primary education.
- The top fifth of the world's population own 86% of global wealth, control 82% of the world market, 68% of foreign investment and 74% of phone lines, while the bottom fifth score just 1% in each of these categories.
- UN figures show that over the last four years, the world's 200 richest people have doubled their wealth to more than $1 trillion ($1,000 billion). The

number of people living on less than a dollar a day (around 70 pence) has remained unchanged at 1.3 billion.

Which figure(s) really surprise you? Why? ❏

b) Many people have needs. Think of the following:

- A starving family in sub-Saharan Africa.
- A couple who have lost their home in flooding.
- A father who has lost his job and with it, his income and self-respect.
- A Christian believer locked away in the jails of an anti-Christian state who has not had fellowship for several years.
- A child who feels upset and disturbed by the effects of her parent's recent separation.
- A claustrophobic who is forced to take a daily journey to work on the Tube.
- A person who is shut-in and has few visitors.
- A wealthy, hard-working manager whose life is full of things yet empty at the core.
- A young Christian who is finding it hard in a non-Christian family situation.
- A wife in a police state who has not seen her husband since he was taken away by the government authorities.
- An elderly woman with chronic arthritis that makes her life agony.

In each case decide what "daily bread" might represent for them. ❏

3) STUDY

Literally this part of the prayer reads, *"Give us this day our bread for today."* Yet beneath these words lies much more.

In order to study this phrase I have found it helpful to divide it into three parts, each focusing on one of the key words *bread*, *daily* and *our*. Finally, I think it is useful to see how bread sometimes symbolizes far more than food or even just the answer to our physical needs.

Part 1) Asking for *bread*

For the people of the ancient Middle East bread was such a staple part of their diet that when you talked about food you often just said "bread".

◉ a) The Bible is plain that food—and everything else we need for living—is something that comes from God. **Read Psalm 104:14–15** and **James 1:17**. But if God can give he can also take away. **Read Leviticus 26:26**. In the world of the Bible, with its droughts and diseases, what do you think was the sort of tone of voice in which people prayed, "Give us today our daily bread"?

- Do we consider ourselves as dependent on God for provision?
- In spite of our technology are we any less dependent on God than the people of the Bible were? ❏

b) In the Old Testament bread was also something that was to be offered to the LORD. **Read Leviticus 24:5–9.**

- The twelve loaves represented the Twelve Tribes of Israel. What do you suppose was the idea behind giving to God something that represented such an important part of your life?
- What would be a comparable gesture for us today? ❏

◉ **c)** In the Bible, God gives bread both "normally" and also in a miraculous way. A key passage on how God miraculously provided bread for his people is found in Exodus 16. The background is that under Moses' leadership God has dramatically brought the Israelites out of slavery in Egypt. However, the people's gratitude soon turns to grumbling and they start moaning that in Egypt they had had "a settled life around pots of meat and where we ate bread until we were full" (a literal translation of verse 3). God's reply to Moses (in verse 4) is along the lines of "I will rain down bread from the heavens upon them".

Read Exodus 16:11–36.

- If you had been one of the Israelites how would you have reacted to the prospect of a barren wilderness ahead for you and your family? Would you have thought (or said), "God will provide!" or "Whose bright idea was this?"
- Think about how God sent the manna. Did the Israelites have to work for it or was it given as a gift? What conditions were attached to it? What couldn't be done with the manna?
- How did the quantities of manna change on the sixth and seventh days? What principle did this enforce?
- Compared with other miracles in the Bible what is unique about the miracle of the manna (see verse 35)?
- Why do you think that a sample of manna was preserved in the Ark (or box) of the Covenant? What would it have represented to an Israelite of a later generation?
- Does anybody have a story of God's provision (miraculous or otherwise) in their own lives that is their personal equivalent of this account?

Note: Although various non-supernatural explanations for the manna have been proposed, none are satisfactory. It is simplest to take it as the text suggests: a special miracle of God's provision. ❏

d) Jews would also have thought of God giving bread/food when they looked forward to the promised coming of God's Messiah. **Read Isaiah 25:6–10.**

- Who is to attend this banquet?
- On earth we ask merely for bread; yet what will be offered us in heaven?
- What other needs are met here in heaven?

Note: For a New Testament reference to this prophecy see Revelation 21:1–4. ❑

⊙ **e)** All the Gospels recount how Jesus miraculously fed many thousands of people in the wilderness. **Read John 6:1–15.**

- What similarities can you see to the account of God giving the manna to the Israelites?
- What differences are there?
- What does this miracle suggest about who Jesus is?
- Why do the crowd react the way they do?

Note:
   1) The reference to the Prophet in v.14 is significant, especially in conjunction with the reference to the Feast of the Passover (v. 4). In Deuteronomy 18:15,18, Moses prophesied the coming of another prophet like himself.
   2) The blessing Jesus used here and in the Last Supper (see Luke 22:19) was probably this traditional prayer offered before food, "Blessed be the Lord, our God, the King of the universe, who has caused bread to spring out of the earth." ❑

Part 2) Asking for *daily* bread

Although there is some doubt about the exact meaning of the word translated as "daily" (it could mean bread *"for tomorrow"*), there is agreement that this is a prayer that looks only a short way ahead.

⊙ **a)** Let's briefly think again about the story of the giving of the manna in Exodus 16.

- Presumably God could have made "long-life" manna so that a once-a-week collecting trip might have been enough. Why do you think he didn't? ❑

⊙ **b)** In the Gospels two contrasting attitudes to the problem of how to prepare for tomorrow are condemned. **Read Luke 12:16–21.**

- Why is this man "a fool"?
- What has he forgotten about the nature of his life?
- What is wrong about building barns?

Now read Matthew 6:25–34.

- What common attitudes towards the future underlie Jesus' warnings here?
- Can you identify with these attitudes?
- What remedy does Jesus recommend? To what does he urge us to look? Why?
- How can we strike a balance between having no concern about the future and taking wise precautions?
- Do you need to hear these words? ❑

◉ c) In Deuteronomy God warns the Israelites through Moses about the dangers that lie ahead in the Promised Land. **Read Deuteronomy 8:7–18.**

- Surely food and prosperity are better than famine and poverty? What is the danger?
- How was the experience of the manna a humbling one? (See v. 16)
- What lessons are there for us as individuals? For us in what is, by global standards, a prosperous culture? ❑

◉ d) Read **Proverbs 30:7–9.**

- What does the writer see as the peril of riches?
- What does the writer see as the peril of poverty?
- Is this a prayer you ought to pray? ❑

Part 3) Asking for *our* daily bread

Again the little word *"our"* presents itself and again we are reminded that we pray as a people not as individuals.

◉ a) Remember the manna passage in Exodus 16? Read **Exodus 16:17–18** again. "So the people of Israel went out and gathered this food—some getting more, and some getting less. By gathering two quarts for each person, everyone had just enough. Those who gathered a lot had nothing left over, and those who gathered only a little had enough. Each family had just what it needed."
    God had just rescued ("redeemed") his people out of captivity in Egypt.

- Now, in the midst of the barren desert, what was distinctive about how he was blessing his people? ❑

b) In 2 Corinthians 8 Paul lays down the principles on which the Corinthian church is to practise generosity. **Read 2 Corinthians 8:10–15.**

- Why does Paul quote Exodus 16:18 here? As Scripture sees the church as the new people of God formed by the "new Exodus" of the cross and the resurrection, what is the point he is making?

(See also Acts 2:44–45 and 4:32–37.) ❑

c) Read **James 2:14–17.**

- What is James criticizing here?
- What criteria would James use to define true faith?
- How might James suggest that at least some people's prayer for "daily bread" might be answered? Does this advice just extend to providing clothes and food for "rough sleepers" and the homeless? Give other examples of how this might work. ❑

Note: One difficult issue that cannot be dealt with adequately in a few moments is what happens when God seems to fail in his provision. What, for example, do we say to the Christian in the developing world who has prayed this prayer but who is still hungry? Three points:

- *This is, of course, part of the whole issue of suffering and to treat it properly would require the consideration of issues such as sin, God's will, how God treats his children, and the devil.*
- *It would be simplistic, heartless and almost certainly incorrect to say that anybody's suffering is because of their lack of faith or their deficiency in prayer.*
- *Perhaps the wisest response is to be less concerned about the theory of suffering and to be more concerned about the practice of trying to alleviate it.*

Part 4) Bread as a symbol for all our needs

I have no doubt that Jesus was expecting his disciples to pray for food both for themselves and for their community. Yet there is more to "bread/food" in the Bible than just nutrition for the body.

⊙ a) **Read Isaiah 55:1–3**

- Is this literally food and drink? If not, what do you think is being offered here? ❏

⊙ b) **Read Matthew 4:3–4**

- Jesus was clearly hungry; but is he being tested only over a matter of food?
- Jesus' response is a quotation of Deuteronomy 8:3. What do you think he meant by it?
- What does it mean to "feed on God's word"? To listen to sermons? To study the Bible using guides like this?! What? ❏

c) In John 6 there is a great deal of imagery about bread. The passage starts with John's account of the feeding of the five thousand and we then read how Jesus stills the storm before the crowd gathers around him again at Capernaum. If you have the time read verses 24–59. If not just read the verses mentioned in the questions noting the general context.

- In verse 32, what does Jesus say is "the true bread of heaven"?
- How is the "bread of life" here similar to the manna? How is it different? (Verses 32–35, 48–52, 58.) ❏

4) SUMMARY

- Are we aware that it is God who supplies our needs? Do we regularly ask him for what we need? Do we thank him for what we receive?
- Are we aware of the fact that we need to be dependent on God on a daily basis for our provision? Do we tend to really only pray for "bread" when we are hungry?

- Some people would see this prayer as applying primarily to physical needs (food, drink, etc). Other people would see it as primarily applying to spiritual needs (salvation, eternal life). What are the dangers of both views? How can we get a balanced view?
- How can we live more generously in practical ways? Do we consider that *we* might be God's answer to someone's prayer for daily bread? ❏

5) STEPPING OUT

Practical suggestions

- Spend time thanking God for his provision of "bread" in every sense for you.
- Think about how you could live in a way that shows a greater trust in God and less in the alternatives.
- Remember the manna that was kept in the Ark of the Covenant as a memorial to 40 years of God's miraculous provision to the Israelites. When did God supply you with "manna"? Is there a danger of you forgetting that? How can you make a lasting memorial to them?
- Review your present list of wants. How can you adjust your spending so that you can give more to those who need daily bread? How can your church or fellowship do more to help? What can you do "to live simply so that others can simply live". ❏

Further study

There are many aspects of God's provision to us that could be looked at further.

i) In the first few chapters of Genesis, God's provision for the human race is an important theme.

Read
- **Genesis 1:29**
- **Genesis 2:9**
- **Genesis 2:15–17**
- **Genesis 3:1–7**
- **Genesis 3:17–19**

- God had given Adam and Eve far more than "daily bread". How did Eve fail to trust God's provision?
- In terms of food, what was the end result? ❏

ii) One of the names of God in the Old Testament is that of *Yahweh yireh*— "The Lord Will Provide." This name is given by Abraham in Genesis 22:14. **Read Genesis 22:1–19.**

- How did God provide for Abraham there? Notice Abraham's faith in 22:8.
- How is this story an extraordinary example of trust in God's ability to provide? ❏

iii) Read 1 Corinthians 4:7.

- What is the alternative to not acknowledging God as the source of all that we are and have?
- What is the danger in not acknowledging him as giver? ❏

Questions to think about

- Why do our *greeds* always exceed our *needs*? What can we do about it? Get more or desire less?
- What is the difference between faith and recklessness? For example, X refuses to pay towards a pension ("God will provide") whereas Y has every sort of insurance policy possible ("God helps those who help themselves"). Which is right?
- Having too much and too little both bring problems. What is the best response to: a) riches in our own lives, b) poverty in the lives of those around us?
- George and Mary both pray the Lord's Prayer regularly. George has a financial crisis but the day before he will have to sell his house, a mystery gift of £5,000 pounds is sent to him. Mary has suffered severe medical problems for years but has somehow been enabled to keep working. Which of these examples of God providing is the one most likely to get talked about? Are both miracles?
- Some people have "bread" (in whatever sense) but neither want it nor enjoy it. Do we thank God for having appetites (in whatever sense) as well as having the things we need to satisfy those appetites? ❏

6) SUPPLEMENTARY MATERIAL

a) The Apostle Paul wrote about God's provision frequently.

Read 1 Timothy 6:6–10.

- How would you summarize Paul's "formula for contentment"?
- What attitudes does he point out as being a threat to contentment? Is the only danger they pose a loss of peace of mind?

Read Philippians 4:6–7.

- What is Paul's advice to those who are tempted to worry?
- How does he say that God will respond to our prayer?
- Do you think God's peace is a substitute for having our prayers answered or something that is in addition to having our prayers answered?

b) In the Old Testament having food is one of the blessings given to those who obey the covenant. **Read Deuteronomy 28:1–5.** Equally not having food is one of the curses given to those that break the covenant. **Read Deuteronomy 28:15–18.**

- Is obedience to God an automatic guarantee to us that there will be food on the table?

c) **Read Matthew 25:31–46 again** and let these words address you again.

- What are the six situations that act as the test cases for faith?
- Why are the righteous ones surprised? What does this tell us about their motives for doing good deeds?
- Why are the unrighteous ones surprised?
- Would our faith stand such a test?   ❏

STUDY 8

Pardon:
Being a forgiven and forgiving people

"And forgive us our sins, just as we have forgiven those who have sinned against us." (Matthew 6:12 [NLT])

INTRODUCTION

The fourth petition of the Lord's Prayer brings us to forgiveness. In some ways, this is the most difficult clause of the prayer and many of us may discover issues here that make us feel uncomfortable. If this petition said only "forgive us our sins", then it would be relatively easy to deal with. However, in the Lord's Prayer this plea has a qualifying clause: "just as we have forgiven those who have sinned against us".

The best way to deal with forgiveness is by looking at both dimensions of forgiveness mentioned in this part of the prayer: God's pardon of us and our pardon of others. These are linked and throughout the New Testament the pattern is that it is *precisely* because God has forgiven us that we are to forgive others. We cannot tackle the thorny issue of human forgiveness without first realizing what God's forgiveness of us in Christ actually means.

The issues raised here are so major that you may feel it appropriate to divide the study into two and spread it over a fortnight based on these divisions. There is certainly enough material for two studies. However, if you do divide up this petition then be careful not to separate what Jesus has joined together. Jesus is at pains to point out (notice Matthew 6:14–15) that we cannot trust in God's forgiveness of us without seriously seeking to forgive others.

Let me end this introduction by giving you a warning. Discussing forgiveness can be like striking a match over an open box of fireworks. You can find that even the most mild and easygoing of people bear grudges and cling on to resentments that go back years. Tread softly! And remember too that what emerges in a study group like this is confidential and not to be misused.

1) STARTER

Announce as early as you can that you will later be asking a volunteer to recount a feud that they watched from the sidelines. As it is vital that the innocent (and the guilty!) are protected they need time to think about how they will phrase it so that all the parties are unidentifiable.

Exercises

1) Divide the participants into two sub-groups which ideally should face each other across the room. Designate one group as the Montagues, the other the Capulets. If you have an aversion to *Romeo and Juliet* you can use any other

term as long as it does not correspond to any other living group, party, creed, clan, etc. Give each person in the group a number so that you have M1, M2, M3; C1, C2, C3, and so on.

Now the first Montague (M1) is to imagine that they have been ignored by a member of the other group at a party. M1 must now suggest an appropriate action towards the first Capulet (C1) to: a) punish them and b) "make sure it doesn't happen again". Whatever the action (a calculated insult perhaps) it must repay the offence with a small "amount of interest". C1, suitably irritated, must then suggest an appropriate counter action towards the second Montague (M2) on the same basis. They, in turn, must suggest an appropriate response towards C2....

Continue backwards and forwards until all the participants have spoken. ❑

2) Put the following words and phrases on separate bits of paper on two plates; one from List A and the other from List B. Each participant must take one from each plate without looking.

LIST A	LIST B
Budgie	Superglue
Cat	Red gloss paint
New BMW	Dustbin
Tortoise	Honey
Engagement ring	Hive of bees
Best suit	Ton of concrete
Piano	Microwave
Photograph of Mother-in-law	Raw sewage
Computer	Hammer
Original Beatles LP	Charity shop
Antique oak chest	Blow torch

Each person must now complete the sentence "I will never forgive him (or her) because... " using the words or phrases they have been given *from both lists*. An example might be "I will never forgive her because she dropped *the goldfish* [a list A item] into the *disinfectant* [a list B item]. ❑

Questions

Discuss *some* of the following:

a) Ask people to admit to the worst thing that they did as a child. How do they feel about it now?

b) Without wanting details ask how many people can think of things that, even after many years, can make them feel uncomfortable. Are their feelings to do with embarrassment or guilt?

c) Who has ever wanted revenge or vindication?

d) Who has ever been in a situation where, when they heard of someone's misfortune, their reaction was a certain pleasant satisfaction that "justice was done" or "they got what they deserved"? ❏

2) SURGERY

Discuss a) and some of the other questions.

a) As forewarned above ask for a volunteer to briefly describe a feud that they watched from the sidelines. Remember: make sure that the innocent (and the guilty!) cannot be identified. What caused the feud? What was the result of it? What, if anything, ended it? ❏

b) Read out the following.

> In the early years of the last century a Turkish officer raided and looted an Armenian home. He killed the aged parents and gave the daughters to the soldiers, keeping the eldest daughter for himself. Some time later she escaped and trained as a nurse. As time passed, she found herself nursing a ward of Turkish officers. One night, by the light of a lantern, she saw the face of this officer. He was so gravely ill that without exceptional nursing he would die. The days passed, and he recovered. One day, the doctor stood by the bed with her and said, "But for her devotion to you, you would be dead." He looked at her and said, "We have met before, haven't we?" "Yes," she said, "we have met before." "Why didn't you kill me?" he asked. She replied, "I am a follower of him who said, 'Love your enemies'."[4]

How do you feel about this story? Encouraged? Mystified? Uplifted? Challenged? Or depressed because you don't think you could do anything similar? ❏

c) Have the group try to think of: i) an instance in which one party (an individual, group or nation) extended forgiveness to a party who had wronged them and ii) an instance in which one party refused to forgive the other. What

---

4. Story told in Geoffrey Wainwright, *Doxology: The Praise of God in Worship, Doctrine and Life* (London: Epworth, 1980), p.434.

difference did the act of forgiveness or the withholding of forgiveness make in each situation? ❏

d) Think of the half-finished sentence: "To forgive is to... " Now look at the following words and phrases.

Make a clean start	Let them off
Face honestly what happened	Bury your head in the sand
Say it doesn't matter	Waive your rights
Take the easy option	Take the hard option
Act as if it's fine	Excuse it
Forget	Try to put it behind you
Pretend it never happened	Go soft
Not hold it against them	Lose face

Now ask the group to talk about:

- which of these words or phrases *do* appropriately complete the sentence "To forgive is to... "
- which of these words or phrases *do not* appropriately finish off such a sentence. ❏

e) Has anyone ever known someone who simply refused to forgive? (Again respect privacy and use anonymity.) How had this affected their life? Were they fun to be with? ❏

f) Hand out copies of old newspapers and get each person to list a case where they think that for someone to forgive another would be difficult. ❏

3) STUDY

This is in two parts. First we look at God's forgiveness of us and then at our forgiveness of others.

Part 1) God's forgiveness of us

◉ a) The Bible is plain that "all have sinned; all fall short of God's glorious standard" (Romans 3:32). But what exactly does that mean? In fact various images are used for sin in the Bible.

Read the following Bible passages and after each one is read decide: i) how sin is being described and ii) what *according to this image* would be needed for the sin to be removed or neutralized.

- **Psalm 51:1,2**
- **Luke 7:40–50** *(note especially verse 41)*
- **Colossians 2:14** ❑

🔘 **b)** The images used in the previous question concentrate on sin as an object that has in some way to be removed or dealt with. There is, however, another set of images in the Bible. Read the following and, after each one, decide in what way sin is being described.

- **Isaiah 53:6**
- **Romans 6:23a and Ephesians 2:1**
- **Romans 7:14,23**
- **Colossians 1:21–22**

- What do these images suggest about the relationship that exists between sinful human beings and God?
- Go over each image in turn and describe, in each case, what would be needed to remove or remedy the result of sin. ❑

🔘 **c)** Now have one or two readers read aloud **Isaiah 53**. This is the last of a series of major prophecies in Isaiah of the coming of a humble servant figure who, by his suffering, will reconcile God's people to himself.

- List the sufferings that are mentioned.
- Identify those passages that indicate that the sufferings of the servant are to be for others.

Note: Any Bible with cross references will show this chapter was widely referred to in the New Testament (for example, Matthew 8:17; Luke 22:37; Acts 8:32–33; Hebrews 9:28; 1 Peter 2:22, 24–25). The other three "servant songs" are Isaiah 42:1–7; 49:1–6 and 50:4–9. ❑

d) Read Mark 10:45 and 2 Corinthians 5:21.

- In the first passage what does Jesus say was the purpose of his coming? Which of the images of sin (see questions a) and b) above) does he refer to in his answer?
- How does Paul say that God dealt with "our sins"?
- How do the ideas in both these verses fit with the teaching of Isaiah 53?
- In the 2 Corinthians 5:21 passage how easy do you find it to replace the words *"our* sin" by *"my* sin"? ❑

e) Remarkably Jesus claimed the ability to forgive sins, not just those committed against him but all sins. **Read Mark 2:1–12.** This is one of the first events of Jesus' public ministry.

- Why is the man brought to Jesus? What do you think his friends are hoping for?
- What is the issue that Jesus addresses instead? Why do you think he does this?
- What is Jesus showing here about himself, his priorities in his mission and his way of dealing with people?
- Is the reaction of the teachers of the religious law justified?
- What does this story show about the necessity of forgiveness?
- Do you think that people today are aware of the need to be forgiven? What do you think would make them aware?

Note: There are other instances of Jesus claiming to forgive sins. See, for instance, Luke 7:48 and 23:43. ❏

f) Read Luke 15:11–32. This story was already partly covered in Study 3 but it is so rich in meaning that it can profitably be looked at again from a different angle.

- In what ways had the younger son broken his relationship with his father? What parallels do you see here to the relationship between the human race and God?
- How do the actions and words of the father show his desire to restore the relationship with the younger son? How is this a picture of God's forgiveness?
- Did the younger son deserve forgiveness? What did he have to do to receive it?
- Think of the two sets of relationships at the end of the story. If that between the younger son and the father is a picture of the relationship of the repentant sinner and God, what does the relationship of the older son and the father represent? With which of the two relationships do you most closely identify? ❏

Part 2) Our forgiveness of others

To do justice to the complex issues of human forgiveness would need more than a single Bible study. This material can only touch on some of the general issues involved in forgiveness. Nevertheless the intention here is to stimulate people into thinking about how they forgive and are forgiven.

◉ **a) Read Ephesians 4:31–32.**

- Think of the phrase "God through Christ has forgiven you". Try to explain what you understand this statement to mean *without* using the words "forgive" or "forgiveness".
- Think of some concrete situations in which "bitterness, rage, anger, harsh words, and slander, as well as all types of malicious behaviour" might occur. Paul suggests that an alternative to these is kindness and forgiveness. What

is the relationship between forgiveness and *not* being bitter, angry, malicious etc?
- Paul orders the Ephesians to forgive. Is forgiveness a feeling? If so, how can it be ordered?
- How can we apply to other people the same standard of forgiveness that God has shown to us? ❏

⊙ b) Jesus taught that his followers were to forgive. **Read Matthew 18:21–35.**

- Why does Jesus tell this story?
- How does the story that Jesus tells convey the seriousness of sin? What can the servant do to pay the king back? How is this like our sin before God?
- Why does the king forgive the servant?
- What does the first servant's action suggest about his response to the forgiveness that he had received?
- How does the king get to find out about what happened? What does this suggest to you about how other people view how we do (or don't) practise forgiveness? Are there specific lessons in this for how Christians can witness to Jesus Christ?
- If the king had been asked to explain why he had thrown the first servant into prison what do you think he would have said?
- What general lessons are there here for us about forgiveness? ❏

⊙ c) Let's turn to the relevant part of the Lord's Prayer: "And forgive us our sins, just as we have forgiven those who have sinned against us."

- Is this phrase a request to God to be merciful to us *on the same basis* as we have been merciful to others?
- Or is it a reminder to ourselves that, if we are to trust in God's forgiveness, we must practise it? ❏

d) Read Matthew 6:14–15.

- Immediately after giving the Lord's Prayer, Jesus repeats the command to forgive. Why do you think Jesus felt the need to repeat this?
- What would we be saying about our own forgiveness by God if we failed to forgive others? ❏

e) Read Matthew 18:15–18. The Sermon on the Mount (of which the Lord's Prayer is a part) is primarily about how we live as individuals. Many of the problems to do with Christian forgiveness come from us trying to apply rules meant for us *as individuals* to the communities (whether the church or society) in which we live. In Matthew 18:15–18 Jesus gives some rules for how the community of believers is to display discipline. This sheds valuable light on the practicalities of forgiveness.

- From this passage what do you feel is the ultimate goal of discipline? Is that consistent with the goal of forgiveness?
- Why do you think Jesus teaches a sequence of disciplining: first private pleading, second small-group confrontation, and finally (if all else fails), public judgement? What is this designed to promote? What lessons can we learn for private forgiveness here?
- Does our personal forgiveness of someone who has hurt us rule out legal or disciplinary action? If no, then what *does* it rule out? ❏

f) Read 2 Corinthians 5:20.

- How is God's forgiveness of us described here?
- What, according to Paul, is the implication of this for how we are to live our own lives? ❏

4) SUMMARY

- Do we believe that God can forgive sins? Do we believe that, if we have accepted Jesus, God has forgiven our sins?
- Do we regularly celebrate and marvel at his free forgiveness of us?
- Do we come to God daily to ask him to forgive us our sins?
- Do we really forgive those who hurt us or do we simply try and forget what happened?
- Are we those who seek to have a ministry of reconciliation in our world?
- Do we rely on the power of the Holy Spirit to help us forgive? ❏

5) STEPPING OUT

Practical suggestions

The most important thing about Jesus' teaching on forgiveness is to apply it. Some of the following activities can be done in the group meeting but it may be easier if individuals do the main one in their own time.

- *Healing personal hurts or guilt*

    i) Make some time available and find a place where you can be uninterrupted. First of all write down on a piece of paper all the things that you are sorry for and that you desire that God forgive you. Pray over them, asking God to show you if there is any way that you can now make amends to those that you have hurt or done wrong to. Where it is possible without causing further hurt, resolve to do what you can to make good the hurt to them.

    ii) Now write down on another piece of paper all the things that have happened to you over which you still bear a hurt or a grievance. Ask God to reveal to you anybody against whom you hold a bitterness and put them on the list. Now ask God to give you the power through his Holy Spirit to help you to forgive. Decide with God's help to seek to live with the consequences of the offences against you without bitterness or a desire for revenge. Now go through the list one by one and make a decision to forgive the individuals one by one. As you pray over these individuals and incidents ask God to show you if there is anything that you can do in these cases to bring healing.

iii) Read Psalm 51:1–15 aloud slowly, letting the words speak to you. Then take both pieces of paper and destroy them permanently. Tear them up, bury them in the garden, put them in the dustbin or burn them. Resolve that, by God's power, you will not revive the matter you have listed on them.

iv) Carry out, as soon as possible, those things that you resolved to do.

v) When in the weeks ahead you remember further hurts or offences then mentally add them to the list and repeat the procedure. If hurts or offences surface that you have already let God deal with, remind yourself that the matter is dead and buried and that you are determined not to revive or dig it up.

- Ask yourself where in your family, community or work-place can you be a reconciler?

NOTE: Some of these matters may not be appropriate for open discussion. ❑

Further study

There are many aspects of God's forgiveness to us that could be looked at further. In the Bible the issue of forgiveness is most clearly dealt with in the letters of the New Testament.

- God's forgiveness of us is the subject of much of the book of Romans; see, for example, Romans 5:8–11.
- Paul deals with some of the many aspects of our forgiveness by Christ in Colossians 2:12–15.
- The Apostle Peter also explains how the cross of Christ brought us forgiveness in 1 Peter 3:18.
- The brief letter of Paul to Philemon is all about forgiveness and reconciliation centred round the conversion and subsequent return to his master of the runaway slave Onesimus. There is an exercise based on the letter to Philemon in the Supplementary Materials section at the end of this study.
- The story of Zacchaeus in the Bible (Luke 19:1–10) illustrates what the effects of repentance and conversion should be: a desire to make recompense and restitution. ❑

Questions to think about

Try to answer some of the following.

- Does being ready to forgive mean that we have to reduce our sense of what is right and wrong?
- Why does revenge seem so much more appealing than forgiveness?
- Which do you find the hardest to forgive? An insult to yourself or an insult to someone you care for?
- There are two extreme ways of confronting sin in someone's life. One is to challenge them directly by pointing out their sin. The other way is more indirect; it is to try and persuade them to recognize their sin themselves. In the first way we act as judge; in the second we try to get them to act as judge themselves. What are the advantages and disadvantages of both methods?
- What is the difference between wanting revenge and wanting to be vindicated?
- Can Christians forgive too readily? For instance, imagine there has been a vicious mugging in your town leaving an old lady in hospital. Is it either right or sensitive for a Christian to say openly that they forgive the muggers?
- What are the dangers in:
  o Delaying in asking God for forgiveness?
  o Overemphasizing our sin and underestimating God's forgiveness?
  o Overemphasizing God's forgiveness and underestimating our sin?
  o Refusing to believe that God has forgiven us but instead hoping that he might forgive us?
- When are feelings of guilt good for us and when are they unhealthy?
- How would you answer the following statements?
  o Christianity's emphasis on sin and guilt is neurotic and leads to psychological unhappiness.
  o Christianity's emphasis on free forgiveness undermines morality.
  o How God forgives us depends entirely on how we forgive others.
- Does forgiveness overflow out of your life or does God have to squeeze it out? How can we learn to live lives where forgiveness comes more easily? ❏

6) SUPPLEMENTARY MATERIAL

a) Paul wrote the letter to Philemon as a personal plea for forgiveness and reconciliation for a third party, Onesimus. Paul could have shrugged his shoulders and said, "It's none of my business", yet he chose to act as a go-between. Are there situations where you can help make peace?

Choose one of the following scenarios and then, either as pairs or as a group, sketch out the points of the "Philemon-like" letter that you would write to the hurt party urging them to forgive. You can assume that, in each case, the injured party is a Christian. None of the scenarios are based on true stories but they all involve complexities. As you sketch out the answer ask what it would mean for the people involved here to exercise real forgiveness.

- Bill and Beverly's son Jack has been ridiculed and insulted at school by the son of another family in the church congregation. As a result Bill and

Beverly now refuse to speak to anyone belonging to the other family who are as upset by their son's behaviour as anyone else.

- Dave is a middle-aged man who has refused to forgive his father for the abusive way he was treated at home. His father is now frail and elderly.
- Jan broke off all links with her daughter who had pretended to leave home to go to college, only in fact to move in with her boyfriend. The daughter is now pregnant, and the boyfriend has walked out.
- Changes have been introduced in the church by its leaders. The older members of the congregation feel betrayed; they think the changes have been introduced too quickly and without consulting them. They are threatening to withdraw their giving and, if the changes are not reversed, to leave.
- Three weeks before he was due to marry Angela, Barry suddenly called it all off and left town to marry someone else. Now, ten years later, the marriage has failed and an apparently repentant Barry has come back and has started to go to the church that Angela attends. She has publicly stated that "if he comes again, I go". ❑

b) Read Psalm 103.

- In what different ways is God's forgiveness described here? ❑

c) Read 1 Corinthians 6:1–8.

- Is Paul saying here that the solution to every dispute is to forgive and forget?
- When, however, does he suggest that it may be best to "accept the injustice and leave it at that". Why? ❑

d) Read Romans 12:17–21.

- Forgiveness has negative (do not do this) and positive (do this) aspects. What does this passage tell us about what we are not to do and what we are to do when we forgive? ❑

STUDY 9

Protection: Battling against evil

"And don't let us yield to temptation, but deliver us from the evil one."
(Matthew 6:13, [NLT])

INTRODUCTION

This petition talks about the battle against evil. In the first part we ask that it we might not give in to temptation; in the second we ask that we may be protected from the evil one, the devil.

Leader's note: When leading this study and selecting the material to be used, it is important that you conclude it on a positive note. Temptation, sin and the devil are serious matters but we must always remember that Christ has won the victory for his people. This is something that is emphasized in the final study so do encourage anyone who misses that study to work through it themselves.

---

1) STARTER

Either do the following exercises *or* discuss some of the questions below.

Exercises

Either

Buy four sugar-coated doughnuts, or some other appropriately sweet and sticky food. Give them to four people and ask them one by one to eat their doughnut *without* licking their lips. To make it harder get the others in the group to persuade them to do just that.

Or

Play the word game *"Yes... No"*. This is the old game designed to see how long someone can answer questions without saying either *yes* or *no*. Choose someone from the group to be the questioner; they should be capable of forceful, rapid-fire questions. Someone else should be designated as time-keeper; they should have a watch, a pen and a piece of paper. Those questioned can either be everybody else in the group or individual volunteers. The time-keeper starts and the questioner then rapidly asks them questions that can be about anything. When they say either "yes" or "no" their turn is finished and the time is noted. The winner is the one who can go the longest without saying either word.

Other than being good ice-breakers, both of these exercises make the point that it can be very hard to avoid doing what you do not want to do. And especially when you are being pressured! ❏

Questions
- What was the most recent test or exam you took? How did you feel about taking it, passing it or failing it?
- What comes to mind when you think of the word "temptation"?
- What is the weirdest superstition you have ever come across?
- Can the group list the seven deadly sins? What would you add to the list today?
- Imagine you want to write a novel with a *really evil person* in it. What would characterize the *really evil person*? When you have listed these features, you might like to ask whether evil is really that obvious. ❏

2) SURGERY

Do the following exercise privately
Spend a few minutes thinking of: a) a situation where you were tempted to do something but gave in and b) a situation where you were tempted to do something and did not give in. *We will return to these later.*

Now discuss some of the following
a) If you were to ask people in the local shopping centre what came to mind when they heard the word "temptation", what answer would you get?

b) Go round the group listing as many temptations as you can think of. Don't be too fussy about what exactly constitutes a temptation. The idea is to get away from the view that temptation is always to do with prohibited sex, shopping or chocolate!

c) If you were trying to define the word *Satan* or *devil* from the popular press, what ideas and images would you come up with? ❏

3) STUDY

This is divided into three parts: the first deals with the nature of temptation and testing, the second with the nature of the devil and the third with the nature of our spiritual battles.

Part 1) Tempting and testing
Note that although this issue of the devil occurs in this section I think it is best to leave discussing him until the next part.

◙ **a) Read Deuteronomy 8:1–5.**
The context of this passage is that, after 40 years in the wilderness, the Israelites are about to enter the Promised Land. As God gives new rules for how the people are to live in the land, he refers to the past.

- What does this passage tell us about God's character?
- What does it tell us about the relationship God has with his people?
- What, according to verse 2, was the purpose of the testing in the wilderness?
- Why, when he is giving instructions about the future to his people, does God refer to the past? ❑

◉ b) For a brief but helpful New Testament perspective on temptation and testing read James 1:2–4.

- What does James see as the purpose of testing?
- How should this affect our attitude to temptation?
- What would you think about a Christian who said, "*I'm* never tempted!"?
- How does the petition in the Lord's Prayer *"don't let us yield to temptation"* fit with James' comment here? ❑

◉ c) Read Matthew 3:13 – 4:11.

- What do you think was the significance for Jesus of the announcement in verse 17?
- In 4:1 we read that "Jesus was led out into the wilderness by the Holy Spirit to be tempted there by the devil". What does this tell you about the roles of God and the devil in temptation? Is it sinful to be tempted?
- What link to the baptism of Jesus do you see in 4:3 and 4:6? What does this suggest the purpose of the temptation was?
- For each of the three temptations summarize the challenge for Jesus and why giving in might have seemed attractive.
- Notice the quotation of Deuteronomy 8:3 in Matthew 4:4. It is not only an appropriate quote for a hungry man; it also suggested that Jesus identified with Israel in the wilderness. How many parallels can you find between Jesus' temptation and the history of the Israelites in the desert as summarized in the Deuteronomy passage that you just looked at?
- During the second temptation the devil quotes Psalm 91:11–12 to Jesus. What lessons can we draw from this?
- Jesus responds to the devil in every case by using verses from the Bible. Why do you think this strategy was successful? Does quoting Bible texts automatically defeat the devil?
- Think of what Jesus was offered by the devil in the third temptation. Now glance at Philippians 2:10–11—"so that at the name of Jesus every knee will bow, in heaven and on earth and under the earth, and every tongue will confess that Jesus Christ is Lord, to the glory of God the Father." On this basis did Jesus lose out by resisting this temptation? Is this an encouragement?
- What was God's intention by allowing this to happen to Jesus? What was the devil's intention? Was this a *testing* of Jesus or a *temptation* of Jesus? Does it depend on whose side you look at it from? How does this help you with the idea of personal temptation?

d) The Gospels record a second occasion where Jesus was strongly tempted. This was in the Garden of Gethsemane on the night before the crucifixion.

Read Mark 14:32–42.

- What is the temptation that Jesus now faces?
- Why do you think he needed the company of friends? What does that suggest about one way we can receive support when we face temptation?
- What evidence do you see of the cost of resisting temptation? (Note that in Luke's account we read: "Jesus prayed more fervently, and he was in such agony of spirit that his sweat fell to the ground like great drops of blood" [Luke 22:44]. Do we know anything at all about resisting temptation to this extent?)
- Why do you think that Jesus warns Peter especially to stay awake and pray? What, in fact, did Peter do within a few hours? (See Mark 14:66–72). ❏

e) The letter to the Hebrews was written to a church that was being tempted to give up the faith and in it there are a number of references to Jesus facing temptation. **Read Hebrews 2:18; 4:14–16.**

- What do you think it means that Jesus "faced all of the same temptations we do" (4:15)?
- How is the fact that Jesus successfully faced the temptations we face an encouragement? ❏

f) Who do we blame for temptation? **Read James 1:13–14.**

- Why does James say that it is incorrect to say that "God is tempting me" when we want to do wrong? Who are we blaming? Who are we excusing?
- Where does James put the real source of human evil?

Now read Mark 7:20–23.

- Where does Jesus put the root of human sinfulness?
- If sin and temptation simply originated from the devil what would we need for it to be dealt with?

- If, however, as Jesus and James teach, sin originates from within us, how is the problem different? What answer is needed to overcome temptation? ❏

Part 2) The devil

Leader's note: Doing a Bible Study about the devil is not easy!

- Although there is a lot about evil and sin in the Bible, the devil himself receives relatively little mention and there is a lot we do not know. Most of the references about him are in passing.
- The silences in the Bible about the devil have often been filled in by folklore and fiction in a way that is generally misleading.
- Practically there is a real danger of exaggerating either the devil's power and authority (leading to fear) or the extent to which he is defeated (leading to overconfidence).
- Although rare, it is possible that someone in the study group will have had a problematic experience (either real or imagined) of the demonic that still troubles them. This is not something easily resolvable in a group setting and it is far wiser to encourage the person concerned to talk privately to a church leader with pastoral experience.

Note: The Hebrew word Satan *means "accuser" or "adversary"; the equivalent Greek word is* diabolos *from which we get "devil" and "diabolic".*

The following three sections deal with aspects of the devil and his work. If short of time, reduce the number of passages discussed in each section rather than eliminating an entire section. In particular, don't omit the third section!

◉ a) The character and nature of the devil
Read out the following passages. After each is read, decide: a) what title or name they refer to the devil by, and b) what they tell us about what he does.

- **Matthew 13:19**
- **1 Thessalonians 3:5**
- **Matthew 12:24**
- **John 8:44**
- **2 Corinthians 4:4**
- **Revelation 12:7–9**   ❏

◉ b) The devil's strategy
Read out as many of the following passages as possible. After each is read, discuss what they tell us about how the devil works.

- 1 Peter 5:8
- 2 Corinthians 4:4
- 2 Corinthians 11:13–15
- 1 Timothy 3:6,7
- Ephesians 2:2   ❏

◉ c) Jesus' defeat of the devil
Read out the following passages. After each is read, discuss what they tell us about how Jesus has triumphed over the devil.

- **Hebrews 2:14**
- **John 12:30–33**
- **Colossians 2:14**
- **1 John 3:7–10**
- **Revelation 20:10**

- Summarize what Jesus did to achieve that victory over the devil.
- Why *practically* is it important that we remember that Jesus has already won the victory over the devil?   ❏

Part 3) The spiritual battle Christians face
◉ a) Read 1 Corinthians 10:12–13.

- What warning does Paul give here to the Corinthians?
- What promise does he give?
- How can this help when giving in to temptation appears to be the only option?   ❏

◉ b) Read Ephesians 6:10–18.

- What do we learn here about the power of the devil's forces? About their strategy?
- Consider the equipment listed; is it for offensive or defensive purposes?
- What phrase is repeated in verses 11 and 13 about the sort of victory that we should be seeking? What does it tell us about our aims in this spiritual conflict? See also **James 4:7**
- What resources are we given by God? What does this mean in practice?
- In this passage Paul makes much of the fact that the power and the armour for battle are from God. What is he anxious to encourage? Discourage?
- A Roman soldier's armour was designed: a) to protect the front not the back, b) to work with that of other soldiers to give a shared mutual protection. What lessons might we draw from these principles for our own spiritual warfare?   ❏

c) Read 2 Corinthians 10:3–5.

- What particular aspect of spiritual warfare is Paul concerned with here?

- Does he consider the devil's hold in this area to be impregnable?
- Where does his confidence come from? ❏

4) SUMMARY

Temptation and testing

- What is the difference between being *tested* and being *tempted*?
- Hypothetically, describe a situation where someone is faced with a desire to do something or to take up an offer. It should be something which, *if they fail*, becomes a temptation that leads them into sin and which, *if they pass*, is a test which leads them to a deeper holiness and knowledge of God.
- What are the short-term and long-term consequences of: a) passing a test and b) giving into a temptation?
- Should we seek to be tempted or tested in order to grow as Christians? Or should we seek to avoid temptation and testing? ❏

The tempter

- Is there a danger of *under*-emphasizing the existence and power of the devil?
- Is there a danger of *over*-emphasizing the existence and power of the devil? How do we keep a balance?
- Why is it vital that we hold on to the belief that Satan has already been defeated by Jesus and that one day he will be totally destroyed? ❏

The battle

- A character in Oscar Wilde's book *The Picture of Dorian Gray* says, "The only way to get rid of a temptation is to yield to it." What alternative advice are we offered in the Bible?
- But are we *just* offered good advice? What help are we given? See 1 John 4:4—"But you belong to God, my dear children. You have already won your fight with these false prophets, because the Spirit who lives in you is greater than the spirit who lives in the world." ❏

5) STEPPING OUT

Practical suggestions

- No part of the Lord's Prayer is theoretical and this is no different. Think through some of the following imaginary situations. In each case, what would you do or advise?
  - A member of your church is in a financial crisis. She is being offered a lucrative job that involves her letting substandard properties to poor people at excessive profits. She feels that it is an answer to prayer.
  - A Christian has committed adultery with a colleague. He says, "God is responsible" because he and the colleague were accidentally booked in to the same hotel room at a conference.
  - A Christian who struggles financially comes to you worried whether they are truly a Christian. They have been told that if they were a *real* Christian they would be "walking in victory" and would know God's financial blessing.

- A Christian business colleague tells you that, in order for a badly needed business contract to be won, their manager wants them to "pad" their CV so it looks like they have more experience. They have been promised that it is a "one off".
- An elderly member of your church tells you that they feel their life has been a failure. They feel that all they have done has been worthless. "I feel like throwing myself off a cliff" they say.
- A dynamic member of the youth group has been offered an excellent job abroad. However, her parents are putting pressure on her to stay at home; they claim she is "giving in to temptation".

- How can we make it *easier* for one another to face temptation? How (presumably unintentionally) can we make it *harder* for others to face temptation?
- For *private consideration*. Remember the situation where you were tempted and gave in and the situation where you were tempted and didn't? Think about them again now. Where in your life are you vulnerable to the devil's attacks? How can you strengthen yourself in that area?
- For *private consideration*. Who do you know in your church who is facing temptation? Pray for them.

You might want to end the study by praying together the ancient Celtic prayer known as the Shield of St Patrick after the fourth-century missionary to Ireland. This is the version paraphrased by Cecil Frances Alexander.

I bind unto myself today the strong name of the Trinity,
by invocation of the same, the Three in One, the One in Three.
I bind this day to me forever by power of faith, Christ's incarnation,
his baptism in the Jordan river, his death on the cross for my salvation;
his bursting from the spiced tomb, his riding up the heavenly way,
his coming at the day of doom I bind unto myself today.
I bind unto myself today the power of God to hold and lead,
his eye to watch, his might to stay, his ear to harken to my need,
the wisdom of my God to teach, his hand to guide, his shield to ward,
the Word of God to give me speech, his heavenly host to be my guard.
Christ be with me, Christ within me,
Christ behind me, Christ before me,
Christ beside me, Christ to win me;
Christ to comfort and restore me;
Christ beneath me, Christ above me,
Christ in quiet, Christ in danger,
Christ in hearts of all that love me,
Christ in mouth of friend and stranger.
I bind unto myself the name, the strong name of the Trinity,
by invocation of the same, the Three in One, and One in Three,
of whom all nature hath creation, eternal Father, Spirit, Word;
praise to the God of my salvation, salvation is of Christ the Lord!

Further study

i) An important passage on the nature of temptation is the story of the rebellion of the first human beings in Genesis 3. **Read Genesis 3:1–24.**

- Remind yourself of the situation that the first human beings were in at the start of this chapter. What had God given them? What did they need?
- What does the serpent suggest about God in verse 1? Is it a direct accusation that God is untrustworthy? What other examples of subtle temptation have you come across recently?
- What do you think of Eve's response in verse 2 and 3? What might have been a better response? What lessons are there here for us in dealing with temptation?
- In verse 4, what does the serpent claim about God's warning about eating the fruit? What does he imply about God's motives?
- What does the serpent claim is actually on offer? Is it true?
- This is the first temptation in human history but it is also the pattern for all subsequent temptations. What principles of temptation can you identify here?
- Look at verses 11–13. What excuse does Adam use? What excuse does Eve use?
- What immediate results of Adam and Eve's failure to obey God can you see in verses 7–11?
- What, in verses 14–24, does God say will be the long-term results of this action? Do these consequences seem severe? What events have you known, or heard of, where a single act of disobedience or sin has affected someone's entire life? What lessons are there for us when faced with temptation?
- Amid the grim announcements of the consequences of their sin, there is one ray of hope. In verse 15 God says to the serpent that the woman's offspring "will crush your head, and you will strike his heel". What do the nature of injuries to the serpent and the male child suggest about the outcome of this future confrontation? This passage is seen as the first prophecy of the coming of Jesus and his victory over the devil through the cross and resurrection. The Apostle Paul refers to this in a promise he gives to the believers in Rome: "The God of peace will soon crush Satan under your feet. May the grace of our Lord Jesus Christ be with you" (Romans 16:20). How could this encourage you when faced with temptation in the future?
- Summarize what you have just learned about:
  o The nature of temptation
  o The one who tempts
  o The consequences of giving into temptation
  o God's way of dealing with our sin

Note: try to ignore all the fascinating issues such as where and when this happened. There are more important issues! ❏

ii) The role of the devil as accuser is well shown in Zechariah 3. **Read Zechariah 3:1–10.**

- What is Satan's role here?
- What does the LORD do to Satan?
- What does he do for Jeshua?
- How does God in Jesus do the same two things for us?   ❑

Questions to think about

- Do we ever pride ourselves on having triumphed over a sin that *for us* is not a real temptation? (C S Lewis once said this was like "eunuchs boasting of their chastity"!) What harm does this do us? What harm does it do those who are struggling with this exact sin?
- Does belief in the devil and the supernatural mean that we have to believe everything that is labelled as paranormal?
- The Bible in general, and the New Testament in particular, concentrates much more on human potential for evil than on the devil. How can this be a lesson for us?   ❑

6) SUPPLEMENTARY MATERIAL

a) Some cautionary words about dealing directly with the devil can be found in 2 Peter and Jude.

- **2 Peter 2:9–11**
- **Jude 8,9**

Although not the easiest passages in the New Testament to understand, both these sets of verses seem to suggest that it is the responsibility of Jesus Christ, not us, to rebuke the devil. What might this mean practically?

Note: The Jude passage refers to a Jewish legend[5] not recorded in the Old Testament. ❑

b) A classic passage about testing is found in Genesis 22:1–18.

Note: a) Although strange and revolting to us, sacrifice of one's firstborn child seems to have been fairly common in the ancient Middle East. b) Isaac was not "just" Abraham's son; God had told Abraham that Isaac was the son through whom all the promises would be fulfilled (Genesis 21:12).

- What is Abraham asked to do here? How do you suppose he felt?
- Why is this a test of his faith and obedience? How are they linked?
- What "double meaning" can you see in verse 8? See **John 1:29.**
- Abraham passes the test. What blessings are given, or confirmed to him, as a result?   ❑

---

5. Apparently the story was found in a document called "The Assumption of Moses" which has since been lost.

Perspective:
Living life God's way

"For yours is the kingdom and the power and the glory forever. Amen."
(Matthew 6:13, footnote [NLT]).

INTRODUCTION

This final phrase of the Lord's Prayer does not appear in the earliest manuscripts of the New Testament and, as a result, most modern translations place it as a footnote. Nevertheless, I think that we should consider it as part of our model for praying. My reasons are as follows:

• If it is an addition to the Lord's Prayer it is very early and comes from the first century.
• Jewish prayers of Jesus' time generally ended with some sort of blessing to God and so therefore it is quite probable that Jesus expected his followers to add an ending like this.
• I think that it is extremely unlikely that Jesus would have expected his followers to end the prayer on the rather downbeat note of "protect us from the evil one". Here, as elsewhere, the devil does not have the last word!
• Finally, this phrase ends our prayers in the best possible way; with praise. It is a model of the exultant, jubilant and hopeful note upon which all our prayers ought to end.

Leader's note: As this is the concluding study and covers a number of very important topics it is slightly different to the previous studies. In whatever way you modify this, it is wise to end this study on a note of praise and encouragement. If you have any sort of musical ability among you then end with a triumphant hymn or song of praise!

---

1) STARTER

Exercise

Do one of the following.

a) Distribute a variety of national newspapers of different dates and types to pairs of people within the group. The group are to imagine that they are part of an alien delegation on their way to make contact with most important and influential people and organizations on Planet Earth. Unfortunately, due to an intelligence failure, the only data you have available is these selected newspapers. In twos, glance through the paper making a list of who and what seem to you to be the key people and organizations. Then spend a few minutes together discussing them. ❏

b) Copy the following names onto different pieces of paper:

- An immigration officer
- The Secretary General of the United Nations
- A new-born baby
- An athlete who won two gold medals in the last Olympics
- An airline pilot
- A successful film director
- The editor of *BBC News*
- The head of the Bank of England
- A member of Parliament
- A heart surgeon
- A high court judge
- A pop singer with three consecutive number-one hits

Each person in the room should take one name. After giving people a moment to think, go round the room asking for each participant to briefly give reasons why the person they represent is the most important. Then ask for a show of hands over which of these people is the most important. You could, if you were well organized, do a proper voting system to determine an overall winner but the issue is not really who wins; it is how you decide who is most important. There are many different issues involved here. ❏

Discuss some of the following

a) You have the possibility of owning a single item from anywhere in the world; it could be a work of art, a car, a piece of electrical equipment, even a national heirloom. Take some time for people to think about what they would choose then go round the group and get people to talk about what they have chosen and why.

b) Describe a time in your life when you were most on an adrenalin "high". What was so exciting?

c) As a child (or as an adult!) what superhero would you have liked to be? Why?

d) What piece of music inspires you? Why?

e) Someone with a negative point of view sees a half-filled glass and says it's "already half empty". In contrast, someone operating with a more positive frame of mind says of the same glass that it's "still half full". Give the two alternative perspectives on the following:

- The achievements of someone who ended their career as a deputy head teacher.
- A writer whose books are praised but never bring them any financial reward.
- A football team who are trailing 1:0 with fifteen minutes to go.
- The weather forecast for your week's holiday: prolonged heavy showers with strong winds.
- Being 45. ❑

2) SURGERY

Discuss some of the following questions

- Who has known someone who had a burning ambition for something, made extraordinary sacrifices for it and finally achieved what they wanted?
- When you were a child how did you envisage the twenty-first century? Have your hopes or fears been realized so far?
- Who has ever lived somewhere where they had to be careful of what they said because of the political or religious authorities who wanted to wield total power? How did it affect life?
- What have you wanted to do but never had the opportunity and resources for?
- What are people's fears about the future?
- Who has known someone who really impressed them? What was it about them that was so impressive?
- What is the most important document you have ever signed, or watched being signed? ❑

3) STUDY

These final words of the Lord's Prayer give the right perspective on the future. This study is divided into five parts. Try to do all the parts even if you don't do all the questions within each part.

Part 1) Yours is the kingdom: the ultimate priority of our lives

By praying "Yours is the kingdom" we are acknowledging that the only priority in our lives should be God's agenda for our world.

◉ a) Read Haggai 1:1–11.
The background to this passage is that in 538 BC the Jews returned from exile in Babylon. By 520 BC, when Haggai began his ministry, the temple still lay in ruins. Ezekiel and Jeremiah had made it plain that the cause of the exile in Babylon was the LORD's anger over his people's neglect of their covenant relationship with him. Nevertheless, God still brought them back to their own land.

- On their return what do you think should have been the priority of the people? Out of what motives?

- What other priorities do they seem to have had?
- Have these other ventures been successful?
- What lessons can we learn from this about our own commitment to God's work? ❑

◉ b) Read Matthew 6:31–33 (we touched on it in Study 7).

- What two groups are contrasted in this passage?
- What is distinctive about the priorities of these two groups?
- What promise does Jesus make to those who adopt the right priority? ❑

◉ c) Read Matthew 16:24–28.

- What is Jesus asking his followers to do? How might someone in your culture and community "take up the cross"? What kinds of loss might it involve?
- What does this tell us about the ultimate fate of those who make their own interests their ultimate priority?
- Put like this, following Jesus sounds like the only sane thing to do. But why do so many people (sometimes even professing Christians) choose to put themselves first?
- *Perhaps more for private thought than public discussion.* What might be "the cross" at work or at home that you would have to bear if you were more completely committed to Jesus? ❑

d) Read Philippians 3:7–11.

- From what Paul says here, and from what you know of his history and his situation at the time of writing (see Philippians 1:13–14), what had he sacrificed in order to make the kingdom of God his chief priority?
- How does he view those things he has lost?
- What is his attitude towards the future?

Leader's note: The slight note of uncertainty in v.11, which is more present in some translations than others, is probably best understood not as doubt, but as Paul expressing an uncertainty as to exactly how, and when, he would be raised from the dead.

❑

Part 2) Yours is the power: the strength of our lives

The best plans and schemes are nothing but good wishes and fine words unless they have the power and strength to be brought into effect. By praying "Yours is the power" we are acknowledging that God is the supreme and ultimate power in the universe.

⊙ a) **Read Hebrews 1:1–3.**

• What, according to this passage, is God's relationship to the universe (vv. 2–3)? What does that say about his power?
• What do we learn about Jesus' involvement in the making and keeping of the universe?
• Where is Jesus now and what power does he have?   ❏

⊙ b) **Read Ephesians 1:19–23.**

• What, according to Paul, has God's power done?
• What rulers, authorities, powers and leaders (other than God) exist in the world that seek to control events?
• How does Christ now relate to these forces? For what purpose does he use this power?
• Why do you think Paul prayed that the Ephesians might "begin to understand" this?
• Read Ephesians 3:20. How might understanding the truth that is expressed in these passages change our lives?   ❏

⊙ c) **Read Mark 10:41–45.**

Note: The background here is that James and John had asked Jesus for the places of honour in the kingdom.

• What do we learn from this passage about how human rulers use their power?
• What principle does Jesus lay down for how his followers are to use power?
• How does Jesus set the example of the right use of power?
• How can we apply this principle in our own lives?   ❏

Part 3) Yours is the glory: the purpose of our lives

God's glory is a major theme in both the Old and New Testaments and justice cannot be done to all that it means here. In this section, there is a need for us to be people whose desire is for God to be given glory in our lives.

⊙ a) **Read Psalm 19:1–4.**

Now read Psalm 29:1–11.
• The passage from Psalm 19 talks about the sun, moon and stars while in Psalm 29 the focus is on a great storm sweeping eastwards in from the Mediterranean. What, in both cases, does the psalm writer see in what we might call "the natural world"?
• What does this suggest about why we should praise God?   ❏

b) **Read 2 Corinthians 3:18.**

"And all of us have had that veil removed so that we can be mirrors that brightly reflect the glory of the Lord. And as the Spirit of the Lord works within us, we become more and more like him and reflect his glory even more."

- What, according to Paul, should result from us maturing in our faith?
- What is the role of the Holy Spirit in this?
- Do other people see God's glory reflected in us? How can we become better "mirrors of God"? ❑

c) Read Revelation 5:6–14.

Note: It is useful to remember that most of the unusual images in Revelation are best understood not as descriptions but as a verbal code. So don't try and visualize a seven-horned and seven-eyed lamb; just realize that "seven" symbolizes perfection and completeness, "horns" means strength and "eyes" mean insight or understanding. So the Lamb (Jesus) has total strength and perfect understanding.

- Why does the Lamb deserve glory?
- If we believe that, as Christians, we will eventually be in heaven giving Christ glory like this, how should that affect how we live here on earth? ❑

Part 4) The triumph of the kingdom

This final phrase of the Lord's Prayer reassures us that the universe is not something with an open-ended and uncertain future.

◉ a) Read Revelation 19:1–9.

Note: See the note on how we understand Revelation in Part 3 above.

- The power of evil here is symbolized as "the great prostitute". What do we learn in verse 2 about what evil has done? What are we told here about the ultimate fate of evil?
- Who is involved with praising God here? What is the theme of their praise?
- Who does the bride represent?
- How does this view of the future encourage you? Give examples of times and places where Christians might find the truth of this passage especially encouraging. ❑

Part 5) Amen: Our agreement and commitment

Amen is a significant little word. A Hebrew word that was brought into the Greek of the New Testament, it literally means "be true" or "may it be so". It signifies far more than this, however.

◉ a) In the Old Testament book of Nehemiah we read how, after the Jews returned from exile in Babylon, there was a financial crisis caused by some members of the community charging loans and mortgages at excessive rates.

Nehemiah called a public meeting to address the matter. **Read Nehemiah 5:9–13.**

- In verses 9 and 10 Nehemiah demands that these unjust practices stop. How do the people reply in verse 12?
- Does Nehemiah simply accept this promise?
- How, in word and action, does he make people realize the seriousness of what they have promised?
- What does *Amen* signify here? Is it just an agreement that what Nehemiah has said is good and true? What according to v. 13b was the actual response?
- What do we mean when we say *Amen* to a prayer? What would be the equivalent to saying *Amen* today if: a) You were making a business deal? b) Buying a new house? ❑

◉ **b)** *Amen* however can be more than mere agreement. Read the very end of the Bible! **Revelation 22:17–21.**
- What is promised in verse 20a by Jesus, "the faithful witness"? Why does John the writer of Revelation respond to this with *Amen* in verse 20? What emotions do you think he is expressing here? ❑

4) SUMMARY AND CONCLUSION

a) The kingdom as the priority of our life

What are our priorities? Imagine drawing a series of concentric circles that represent your life. The innermost circle contains those few things, or that one thing, that you are passionate about; this represents your chief priority and is the "kingdom" that you are really working for. The next circle out represents the things that you are quite interested in, and the next beyond represents things that you are merely moderately positive about. There would, of course, be other circles beyond that, but let us just think of these first three.

- *For private thought:*
  o What occupies the inner circle of our lives? Our career, family, hobbies?
  o Where in this diagram does the kingdom of God lie for us?
- *For discussion:*
  o What would it mean to have God's kingdom as the central priority of our lives?
  o How can we help each other to make God's kingdom more central in our lives?

Note: You can do this on your own later as a private exercise with a piece of paper to help you. ❑

b) God's power as the strength of our lives

What strengthens or comforts us when we are challenged by some difficulty? Our friends, our family, our bank balance, our inner determination, our abilities?

- *For private thought:*
  - o What do we trust in when we consider the future? Does it take the place of God?
- *For discussion:*
  - o How can we trust more in God's strength in our lives?
  - o How can we help each other to make God's strength, not our own resources, the thing that we rely upon? ❏

c) God's glory as the purpose of our lives

Although we may disguise the fact, deep down inside most of us like recognition, status, praise and honour. We certainly object when our contribution has been overlooked!

- *For private thought:*
  - o If God told you to take up a job or a career that would involve you in being totally forgotten or ignored by the world around you, would you *willingly* take it?
  - o Is there anything you are involved in, where it is appropriate for you to give God more credit and glory?
- *For discussion:*
  - o Is God's glory and honour a major focus of our lives?
  - o How can we encourage each other to be more concerned about God's praise and glory and less about our own? ❏

d) The triumph of the kingdom

- If we weren't sure about God being king of the kingdom, being all powerful, or being glorious, how would that affect our praying?
- How does the idea that one day God's kingdom, power and glory will suddenly and permanently come, affect our view of our successes and failures?
- How do you feel that hearing Christians pray "For yours is the kingdom and the power and the glory forever" sounds to: a) tyrants, b) businesspeople with their eye on world domination c) the devil?
- How should we *feel* when we pray "For yours is the kingdom and the power and the glory forever"? ❏

e) Amen as our agreement and commitment to God's way of living

- Whenever we pray in church, everybody always says "Amen" automatically. Should we encourage people to think about what they are agreeing to saying first? Should we even encourage people to stay silent if they cannot agree or support what is being prayed?

- As a group go back over this prayer, identifying what, by saying "Amen", you have agreed to.

And finally...

Say the Lord's Prayer together with a pause after each of the lines, and end with a loud *Amen* to show your agreement.　❏

5) STEPPING OUT

Practical suggestions

- Think about "For yours is the kingdom and the power and the glory forever. Amen". Make a point of thinking about it in both good and bad times in your life.
- Watch out for times in your life when you give people or things praise. Give God the praise and glory at the same time; after all, he made everything.
- Repeatedly remind yourself that by saying "Amen" to this prayer you have made a solemn agreement to live according to its principles.
- What situations do you think you might face in the next week or so, in which it will be important for you to remember what you have learned from this study? Prepare yourself in advance.
- What difference do you think you would make in your home, community or workplace if you lived out this prayer consistently?
- Who do you know who knows this prayer but doesn't know the reality of the God to whom it is prayed? Pray for them now, that, whenever they pray it, they would stop and think about what they are praying.
- Either get a loose-leaf folder or create a word-processing document on a computer with the following divisions or headings in it: *Praise, Purpose, Provision, Pardon* and *Protection*. Under these headings put down specific points for prayer or praise on a regular basis and use them to guide your praying.　❏

Further study

i) God's kingdom
Read Luke 9:57–62.
In this passage Jesus teaches that the priority of the kingdom is such that we must follow him: a) without counting the cost (v. 58), b) without delay (v. 59b; the father was presumably still living), and c) without looking back (v. 62).

- Create three imaginary situations in which each of these demands proves to be the real challenge to the follower or would-be follower of Jesus.
- Which of these three is the most difficult challenge for you?

ii) God's power
There are many New Testament references to God's power, especially in Paul's letters. Read some of the following passages. In each case ask: a) who is it that possesses the power? and b) what is the power for?

- **Romans 1:16**
- **1 Corinthians 1:18**
- **1 Corinthians 1:24**
- **1 Corinthians 2:4**
- **1 Corinthians 4:19**
- **1 Corinthians 6:14**
- **2 Corinthians 12:9**
- **2 Corinthians 13:4**
- **Ephesians 6:10**
- **Philippians 4:13**   ❑

iii) God's glory
First read Isaiah 45:20–23 then read Philippians 2:5–11.

- In verse 6 Paul contrasts Jesus with the first human beings. What did Christ do that Adam and Eve didn't? (See Genesis 3:5.)
- What instances can you remember from Jesus' life where he showed his humility? If God can be humble, why do humans find it so easy to be proud?
- In verse 8 the cross is described not as being agonizing, although it was, but as being the ultimate in humiliation. What aspects of crucifixion would have been especially humiliating?
- Look at verses 10 and 11. What do these tell us about Jesus' position now and in the future?
- If Jesus is, among other things, the model for how we are to live a life pleasing to God, what lessons can we learn from these verses about how to value success or fame?
- One of the things that people in this generation really distrust is authority. How could we use these verses to speak to someone who distrusted the idea of an all-powerful God?
- What kind of *kingdom* does this king rule over if his throne is a cross?
- How does he exercise his *power* if he takes the form of a servant?
- Where do we really see the *glory* of Jesus?   ❑

Questions to think about
- What would you say to someone who said that they were scared about God being all powerful because they thought he might be like a "cosmic tyrant"?
- Faced with the hostile non-Christian forces around us we can either concentrate on our present struggles or our future triumph in Christ. What is the danger in *solely* concentrating on either on its own, rather than both together?
- What would you say to someone who said that they weren't sure that God's kingdom was that attractive an option for the future?
- How would you answer someone who questioned why God always wanted to receive glory from his people, from angels and from creation? How would you describe God's glory to them?
- Should we think more about what we say "Amen" to?   ❑

6) SUPPLEMENTARY MATERIAL

a) Revelation 11:15–18.

> Then the seventh angel blew his trumpet, and there were loud voices shouting in heaven: "The whole world has now become the kingdom of our Lord and of his Christ, and he will reign for ever and ever."
> And the twenty-four elders sitting on their thrones before God fell on their faces and worshiped him. And they said,
> "We give thanks to you, Lord God Almighty,
> the one who is and who always was,
> for now you have assumed your great power
> and have begun to reign.
> The nations were angry with you,
> but now the time of your wrath has come.
> It is time to judge the dead and reward your servants.
> You will reward your prophets and your holy people,
> all who fear your name, from the least to the greatest.
> And you will destroy all who have caused destruction on the earth."

If the New Testament tells us that the kingdom of God is currently at war with the devil's forces, then it also states that, one day, God will triumph.

- What is the triumphal announcement in Revelation 11:15? What does it tell us about the extent of God's victory?
- What, according to the song of thanksgiving in verses 16–18, will the final coming of the kingdom involve? What will this mean for those who have rebelled against God? For those who have suffered for the kingdom?
- Is this the ultimate answer to our prayer of "your kingdom come"?

b) Matthew 5:3–11.

- What would our lives look like if we put God's kingdom first?
- In Matthew 5:3–11 Jesus gives us the answer.

c) God's glory
i) Have at least some of the following passages read out and, after each, discuss briefly what each tells us about the glory of God.

- 1 Chronicles 29:11–12
- Psalm 24:7
- Isaiah 42:8   ❑

ii) Read at least some of the following passages.

- Exodus 33:18–23
- Exodus 40:34–35
- 1 Kings 8:11
- Ezekiel 3:22–23

- Moses, the priests and Ezekiel were all godly people. Nevertheless, what was their reaction to the presence of God's glory? (See also Isaiah 6:1–6.)
- Does the thought of God's glory produce a similar reaction in us? Should it? ❏

d) Christ's glory
i) Read the following passages from John's Gospel.

- John 12:23–28
- John 13:31–32
- John 17:1–5

- In these passages in John 13 and 17 Jesus talks about a time when he will enter into his glory. From these passages what event marked the start of this glorification?
- What does this mean for our understanding of glory? What does it say about what we should seek in our own ambitions?
- How does **John 1:14** sum up the disciples' experience of Jesus? ❏

ii) Read Hebrews 2:9.

- What is Christ's status now?
- Why is he *crowned with glory and honour*? ❏

e) The glorious future
Both the Old and New Testaments look forward to a time when God's glory is revealed in its full splendour. The following passages give some indication of the Bible's teaching about the future.

- Isaiah 66:18–19
- Habakkuk 2:14
- Romans 8:18,21
- 1 Corinthians 15:43
- 2 Corinthians 4:17
- Philippians 3:21
- Colossians 3:4

APPENDIX

Practicalities of setting up and leading a small-group Bible study

This Appendix expands some of the comments in the Introduction specifically in connection with the setting up and leading of a study group using material such as these studies.

SETTING UP A GROUP

I suggest that you need the following.

First, you need some measure of three vital things that can't be touched or seen: faith, enthusiasm and commitment. You have to have the *faith* that the Bible is God's written word and that God the Holy Spirit can speak through it into people's lives today. You need to have the *enthusiasm* to get a group going. You also need the *commitment* to ensure that it stays going.

Second, you need participants, a venue, a leader and a host.

- The *participants* raises the issue of how big should a group Bible study be. It is hard to give strict numbers but the general rule is between six and twelve people. The group needs to be large enough that no one feels that they *personally* have to answer every question; but it needs to be small enough so that everyone is challenged to think. What do you do if you regularly get over ten or twelve? First, thank God. Second, consider dividing into two and starting another group. But supposing you have more than twelve participants but don't want to divide up just yet? Well, one option is for everybody to meet together for refreshments and perhaps an opening prayer first and then to divide into separate rooms for study before coming back together again at the end.
- The *venue* should be a setting where people can feel comfortable. After all, the demands the Lord's Prayer makes may be uncomfortable enough. The ideal situation is a cosy room in a home with an ample supply of soft chairs, refreshments and biscuits. If phones can be diverted and shouting toddlers occupied elsewhere, so much the better.
- The *leader* is critical. *Someone* needs to be designated to be in charge; without leadership you are all too likely to get side-tracked. You could decide on a leader for the whole course or you could have an alternating leadership. The easiest solution is to find someone with a gift of leading a study and let them lead all ten studies. Here though—as so often—the easiest solution may not be the best one. I suggest that (perhaps the first two studies) you try and rotate the leadership among those willing "to have

a go". There are several reasons for this. One is that doing it this way helps build confidence among the members of the group. Another is that by doing this you have a great way to identify and train new leaders. After all if, in the future, your group is going to grow by division, then having extra leaders will be essential. The role of the leader is vital and I have included some guidelines below.

- You also need a *host*. Yes, a leader and the host can be the same person but it is better if they are different people. It is almost impossible to make the refreshments, open the door, take phone calls *and* lead the study.

Third, you need Bibles and study questions.

- The first issue with *Bibles* is the potentially contentious one of which translation to use. As I mentioned in the Introduction these studies were written around the text of *The New Living Translation* (British text: Tyndale UK, 2000). Nevertheless, other modern versions such as the NIV, NRSV and GNB should be perfectly satisfactory. The problem with the King James (or Authorized) Version is that its language is so far removed from modern English that to quote or read from it often requires a further act of translation! I suggest that you try to standardize on no more than two versions and make sure that it doesn't become an issue. The second thing is to make sure that you have some spare Bibles available for guests (or the forgetful). And if you are buying some for a study group do try and go for ones with sensibly sized print.
- The *questions* in a Bible study serve two functions. Obviously they should make people think and even the most familiar passages appear in a fresh way. Yet in addition they should provide direction for the way the Bible study is to go. Without specific, written-down questions it is virtually certain that a group will get bogged down, side-tracked on peripheral matters or end up going round in circles. One of the advantages of study guides like this is the hard work of writing questions has been done for you. It is easier if everyone has access to their own copies of this study guide. If people do not have their own copy then the leader will often have to repeat the questions and, as time is at a premium, this is a distraction. There are at least two benefits to everybody having their own study book. First, it allows for preparation *before* the study and if people are prepared beforehand then this will greatly help the study. Second, it allows for the follow-up *after* the study. The way these studies are structured means that it is almost certain that there will be material that the study has not been able to cover. If the participants can tick off what has been done they can think over the extra material at their leisure. Some people may find jotting down thoughts and comments in the study-book margins helpful.

SOME SPECIFIC ADVICE ON LEADING THESE STUDIES

I have outlined the basic components of the sections in the Introduction. Here let me make some comments for leaders.

Starter

The main purpose of this section is to put people at ease and act as a conversational warm-up. Hopefully some of the points that emerge during this time will be addressed later but if they aren't, don't worry. You may also find that just one question is enough to light up a lively conversation. If it does, then stick with it. I recommend that no more than ten minutes is spent on this section.

Surgery

This section focuses in on some of the specific problems that the study section of the Lord's Prayer addresses. Normally I would expect issues raised here to surface later in the study. I would however allow no more than ten minutes for this.

Study

This is the heart of the study and is the section that occupies most of the time. It is also the one on which the biggest decisions will have to be made by the leader. It is certain that you cannot do all the material in an hour so as leader you will have to be responsible for picking, choosing and—if needs be— modifying the questions. The sections marked with ◉ are those I consider to be essential. Even within these sections though there are issues of, for instance, how many questions or verses you should look at. As ever I have tended to give more material than is needed so you may find that you can make do with less. Do remind people that extra material can be studied at leisure later; they can tick off the material that has been already done. For this study section I would suggest that a maximum of 60 minutes is allowed.

Summary

This is a short review section. The task of the leader here is to draw out some general conclusions from the passages studied. To do this well you will have to have been listening to what people have been saying. For this summary I suggest that you allow at least ten minutes.

Stepping out

The best rule here is for the leader to try and stimulate. The aim is for people to leave stimulated by the challenge of what they have been studying. Sensitively try and apply the most relevant of these suggestions and questions to the group. In some cases there are no easy right answers. You should try to allow at least five to ten minutes for this. Remember that good Bible studies don't end when the Bibles are closed. In fact you could argue that this is when they in fact really *begin*.

In terms of overall pacing of the study my advice would be not to worry about having too much time. That's very unlikely and there is always the supplementary material that you can bring in.

In a separate section at the end of each study I have put supplementary material. The extent to which you use this material depends on how long your group spends on each study. If you have a group that moves quickly through the set passages then I suggest that the leader prepare some of the supplementary material. Some people may also find it helpful as "homework" or as a source for private study. Group members can also use the tick boxes to mark material that they have studied so that they can study the rest in their own time.

Whether you use the supplementary material provided at the end is up to the group leader. A good idea would be to prepare the passages and, if you find that you have time, to bring them into the study. Alternatively if you find that you are short of time they can be put to one side and participants could look at them at their leisure.

SOME GENERAL ADVICE ON LEADING BIBLE STUDIES

All the comments I made in the Introduction about participation in Bible studies especially apply to leaders. There are however some special things that I want to say to you. First of all as a general point remember you don't have to be a spiritual or intellectual giant to lead a small-group Bible study. Actually it helps to be ordinary; the best leaders are those who can stay in the background, supply the questions and keep a study on track and on schedule. It is even better to be humble too and a servant of all.

Now let me give you some bits of advice.

Pray!

It is good to begin and end the study with prayer. How exactly you do this is up to you and it may take time for the right pattern to emerge within your group. A typical format would be for either you or someone else to open with a short prayer specifically asking God's blessing and help for the study. Then at the end you could have a longer more open time of prayer. This might involve points raised by the study as well as items for prayer and praise. It is also good to encourage prayer in the intervening week for the study group.

Do your homework!

Other people may be able to come to study cold; a leader shouldn't. Make sure that you have read the passage, checked over the questions and read the notes that I have put in for the leaders. There are decisions you need to make; for example, which of the supplementary passages are you going to study? Which of the optional starter questions are you going to use? The study leader needs to spend time beforehand on the material. There are lots of good background articles and books that you can read to help you. You may find my book on the Lord's Prayer (*God's Priorities: Living Life from the Lord's Prayer* [Kingsway, 2001]) helpful, it uses the same divisions of the Lord's Prayer as used here. Let me say here these particular studies were written during 2001 for a UK audience, a fact inevitably reflected in some of the illustrations and in some of the questions. If you are using these studies for another culture (or even a particular British sub-culture) it should be relatively easy to modify questions to make them more appropriate and relevant for your own setting. You may also want to insert extra questions to address specific issues in your own culture.

Stimulate but don't dominate

The ideal Bible study is where everybody contributes. Your task as leader is to facilitate this; you are to be a catalyst, not a lecturer. This role may involve gently directing questions to those who are hesitant to speak, or encouraging them to elaborate their hesitant answers. It may also involve gently discouraging those who subconsciously (or consciously!) want to dominate the group. Your own aim should be to be unobtrusive. The truly great Bible-study leader is one who leads so well—and in such a low-key way—that the participants don't even notice that they are being led.

Work hard

Leading a Bible study properly allows for little relaxation. You need to constantly listen to what people are saying. Someone may make a comment that needs development; that may be the cue for you to ask them to expand it. Sometimes it is the non-verbal language that is important; the twisting of the fingers that suggests that someone really wants to say something or the stiff back and distant stare that reveals that someone is feeling threatened by the discussion.

Be sensitive

This is particularly important with these studies on the Lord's Prayer. Here, as we study the word of God, we must expect that God's Spirit may convict us in a way that we find uncomfortable. Sometimes it may become evident that some people are finding the questions or comments painful. What do you do? I think the issue is whether it is God or a human being that is doing the hurting. The temptation is always to soft-pedal on some of the more demanding Bible passages, yet the last thing you want to do is dilute what God is saying to someone. For some people it may be that it is the study rather than the Spirit that is doing the hurting. In this case you may feel it right to move on and to try and have a private conversation later. In the back of your mind you may want to ask yourself, "What counselling resources can I draw on if this subject raises deep issues in someone's life?" There are also practical matters to watch. For example, never get the group to read round a passage unless you are sure that no one has a problem with reading aloud. People with dyslexia or a literacy problem can easily be embarrassed this way.

Be patient

Sometimes it can seem to take for ever before anyone answers a question. Resist the temptation to answer it yourself unless it is *absolutely* necessary. If no one wants to answer the question then try and rephrase it or break it down into components.

Stay focused

The general rule is this: know *where* you want to go and *when* you want to get there, and then go for it. Don't get side-tracked. Now to do this you may have to put your foot down in places. One person may want to have a learned theological discussion; someone else may want to bring in a rambling anecdote of little relevance. Try and bring things back on course and here tact and humour often helps. There is, however, an important exception to this rule of being goal-focused. That is where something emerges that is clearly so important that you feel it would be irresponsible to terminate the discussion. Almost certainly this will not be a purely intellectual question—whether angels do have wings can definitely wait until heaven—but it will be one that is a heartfelt burden. Now if this is the case then a *brief* diversion may be justified.

Aim for a good spirit

Positively, that means trying to get people to interact with each other in a friendly and loving way. Negatively, it means damping down any awkward or inappropriate interactions. For example, try not to let the discussion get hijacked by arguments over Bible versions, church structures or other secondary issues.

Enjoy it!

Biography

J.John is widely regarded as one of the most creative Christian speakers in the UK. His much-loved art of storytelling helps us discover God and spiritual meaning – in a way that makes more sense, too, of everyday life.

He is Killy's husband, and father to Michael, Simeon and Benjamin. He loves God and his family, and enjoys food, films and fun.

He lives in Chorleywood, Hertfordshire, UK.

If you would like more information, please contact:
The Philo Trust
141 High Street
Rickmansworth
Herts
WD3 1AR
United Kingdom

or visit www.philotrust.com

ISBN 1 85424 514 7 (UK)
ISBN 0 8254 6015 8 (USA)

ISBN 1 85424 513 9 (UK)
ISBN 0 8254 6014 X (USA)

A Box of Delights

An **A–Z** of the funniest, wisest and most poignant stories, proverbs, jokes and one-liners

Compiled By

J.John & Mark Stibbe

ISBN 1 85424 547 3 (UK)
ISBN 0 8254 6027 1 (USA)